Benjamin Franklin DeCosta

Rambles in Mount Desert: with sketches of travel on the New England coast, from isles of Shoals to Grand Menan

Benjamin Franklin DeCosta

Rambles in Mount Desert: with sketches of travel on the New England coast, from isles of Shoals to Grand Menan

ISBN/EAN: 9783337208332

Printed in Europe, USA, Canada, Australia, Japan

Cover: Foto ©Andreas Hilbeck / pixelio.de

More available books at **www.hansebooks.com**

RAMBLES

IN

MOUNT DESERT:

WITH SKETCHES OF TRAVEL

ON

THE NEW-ENGLAND COAST,

FROM

ISLES OF SHOALS TO GRAND MENAN.

BY B. F. DeCOSTA,

NEW YORK:
A. D. F. RANDOLPH & CO.
BOSTON: A. WILLIAMS & CO.
1871.

Preface.

The substance of this book was originally prepared in the form of a series of letters for the public press, but it was finally decided to give the topics treated a more permanent place in literature. The Author was encouraged to do so, for the reason that the field was unoccupied, no one having attempted to bring out a work of this character relating to what is universally conceded to be the most romantic and interesting portion of the New-England Coast.

This work is not offered as a guide, though the Author hopes that it may not prove unacceptable as a companion. Being popular in its character, it was not thought expedient to cumber the pages with many references, yet it is believed that no important statement of fact is in any case given that does not rest on good authority, unless it be the representation given of Argall.

Stuyvesant Park, New York, 1871

Contents.

Chapter I.	. . . .	Bird's-Eye Views.
Chapter II.	. . . .	Mount Desert.
Chapter III.	A Rainy Morning with the Jesuits.	
Chapter IV.	A Rainy Morning with the Jesuits.	
Chapter V.	. . . .	Somes' Sound.
Chapter VI.	. . . . . .	Among the Mountains.
Chapter VII.	. . . . . .	Among the Mountains.
Chapter VIII.	. . . .	The Lake Region.
Chapter IX.	. . . .	Beach Rambles.
Chapter X.	. . . .	Frenchman's Bay.
Chapter XI.	. . . . . .	Fog and its Effects.
Chapter XII.	. . . . . .	Fish and Fisher-Folk.
Chapter XIII.	. . . . . .	The Isles of Shoals.
Chapter XIV.	. . . .	Penobscot Bay.
Chapter XV.	. . . .	Grand Menan.
Appendix.	. . . .	

Mount Desert.

BIRD'S-EYE VIEWS.

CHAPTER I.

THE COAST — ITS BEAUTIES — ITS PECULIARITIES — ITS RIVERS — THE NORTHMEN — CABOT — VERRAZZANO — GOSNOLD — PRING — DE MONTS — WEYMOUTH — POPHAM — HENRY HUDSON — THE JESUITS.

EVERAL summers ago we were sitting at an open window, looking out upon one of the pleasant parks of New York, vainly endeavoring to detect some perceptible motion among the tall maples whose leaves had hung ever since morning as immovable as foliage cut in cold stone. But not a bough waved nor a leaf stirred, for the dog-days had set in, and a Canicula of unequalled intensity seemed fairly to weigh down the whole world. It was almost impossible to breathe, and the very grasshopper was a burden. Under the circumstances, the mind recurred to every conceivable refuge, and was tantalized by visions of far-off isles, sown like gems in the sea, where, as the bard of Scio imagined, the shrilly-breathing Zephyrus was ever

piping for the refreshment of man. At last fancy found expression in words, and we fell into a serious discussion of the merits of ocean and shore, and resolved to get out of the suffocating city without delay. But where should we go? Of course, repetitions of New York were suggested; and yet what real advantage should we find in any change that gave no fresh mental and moral air? The sickly dilutions of Long Branch would not suffice. And so (I hardly know how it came about) *Maine* was talked of. But what was there in Maine? We certainly did not want to go to Moosehead Lake at this season, to be devoured by black flies. Why, of course, there was "Mount Desert." The name was a novelty, and reminded us of the scenes which suggested the story of "The Pearl of Orr's Island." We at once looked up the place, and found, in several books of travel, brief references, by out-of-the-way tourists, to a wonderful isle off Penobscot Bay, an isle seen in early times[1] by sailors,

(1)—Many into whose hands this book may fall, will doubtless be glad to have here a few additional items on the early history of Maine, which are therefore given in the form of notes, to be skipped by the general reader. First, it must be observed that the pre-Columbian discovery of America is now regarded as an established fact. The authenticity of the Icelandic histories has been amply vindicated, and it is clear that the Atlantic Coast lying above the forty-first parallel was more or less familiar to the Icelandic navigators. Yet the shores of Maine are not mentioned in any of the Sagas. The principal voyages of which we have historical accounts were made to a locality called *Hop*, near the southeastern part of Massachusetts, for which place they laid their course when leaving the headlands of Nova Scotia. Consequently, while the shores of Labrador and Nova Scotia are delineated with considerable minuteness, nothing appears to apply to the coast of Maine.

Biarne, son of Heriulf, who was driven upon the American coast in the

and which was called "Mount Desert." It was a perfect *terra incognita* to our minds; but we at once resolved on an exploration. From Williamson's unreliable and yet invaluable book on Maine, we learned year 985, doubtless saw this part of the country, and the early voyagers probably came thither in their expeditions to obtain timber; but the history of Maine was nevertheless almost a blank as late as the beginning of the sixteenth century. About five years after the re-discovery of America by Columbus, the Cabot brothers sailed southward along the coast of Maine, though without leaving any memorial. In 1504 the Biscay fishermen are known to have frequented the neighboring seas; while in 1524 Verrazzano coasted these romantic shores, being followed the next year by Stephen Gomez, who in the course of this voyage became acquainted with the Hudson River, naming it River of St. Anthony. Among others who visited this region about this period was the Frenchman John Allfonsce, a pilot of Roberval. About the year 1542 he sailed south, and found a great bay in latitude 42° N., which, in all probability, was Massachusetts Bay. A copy of his map of the coast, made from the original, is in the possession of the writer, for whom it was made by M. Davezac. But when we come down to 1602, Gosnold gives us more definite descriptions.

This navigator sailed from Falmouth, England, March 26, came in sight of the coast of Maine May 4, in about the 43d degree of north latitude. The land seen by him may have been Agamenticus, though some persons offer the opinion that it was Mount Desert. In this region Gosnold met eight Indians in a shallop, which they probably had obtained of some Biscay fishermen.

June 7, the year following, Martin Pring came in sight of the coast, and afterwards explored the entire seaboard. The accounts which he gave on his return were reliable and exact.

In the winter of 1604-5, De Monts with his party, who came from France in the preceding May, lived on an island in the St. Croix River. In the spring, De Monts, attended by Champlain and other gentlemen, coasted southward in a small vessel, erecting a cross at the Kennebec, and taking formal possession of the territory in the name of the King of France; notwithstanding the voyage of Pring, according to the views of that age, gave to the English Crown a prior right, Champlain went as far south as Cape Cod, where he was wounded in a fight with the Indians. The map of the coast drawn by him was the most exact of any hitherto made; still it was sufficiently obscure.

In May of the same year, George Weymouth came out with an expedition under the patronage of the Earl of Southampton, the friend of Shakespeare, something of the general features of the whole coast, and decided to take all the principal points on the way from the Isles of Shoals off Portsmouth Harbor, to

and on the seventeenth of the month reached an island on the coast, which he called St. George. This island was probably Monhegan. He afterwards explored the country, and then returned to England, carrying with him several Indians whom he kidnapped for the purpose.

In 1607 George Popham attempted to found a colony at Sagadahoc, where a fort and various buildings were erected. His first thought was to commence his colony on Stage Island, but he afterwards removed to the peninsula. It is claimed, though with no very strong reasons, that this was the first attempt to colonize the coast of Maine. But in all such claims local pride is liable to overreach itself. This colony at Sagadahoc was composed chiefly of persons more or less attached to the Church of England. They brought their chaplain with them, and held Divine Service here on the coast of New England, thirteen years before the Plymouth Pilgrims landed on the shores of Cape Cod. As is well known, after making a fair beginning, they were obliged to give up the enterprise and return to England. Thus it will be seen that popular notion, which makes the Plymouth Pilgrims the pioneers on an unknown coast, has little support in fact. The coast for nearly a hundred years had been tolerably well known, while they fell upon it by mistake, having originally laid their course for the Hudson River.

The history of the Maine coast is yet to be written by some person possessing ampler materials than are yet in hand, and with broader sympathies than any heretofore displayed.

The colony established in 1604-5 by De Monts, at Port Royal, was abandoned, but in 1611 it was re-established by Poutrincourt, who brought over Father Pierre Biard, a Jesuit Professor of Theology at Lyons, and Father Masse. The next year the Marchioness de Guercheville, the warm friend and patron of the mission, induced De Monts to surrender his patent, when it was conferred upon her by Louis XIII., who added all the territory in America between the St. Lawrence and Florida, with the exception of Port Royal, which had been previously confirmed to Poutrincourt. In 1613 the Marchioness prepared to take full possession of her territory in America. Le Saussaye commanded the ship that was sent out, and with him went Fathers Quentin and Lallemant, and Brother du Thet. Arriving at Port Royal, they found Fathers Biard and Masse. A very short time afterwards they left Port Royal in the "Honfleur," to establish a colony at Mount Desert. This was eleven years after Gosnold began his settlement at Cuttyhunk, and seven years before the Pilgrims landed at Plymouth.

Grand Menan, another isle of wonders, lying in the mouth of the Bay of Fundy.

Organizing our small force, we started for Boston, from whence we finally reached the famous Isles of Shoals, which glitter in the sea in sight of Rye (New Hampshire) Beach. At the "Shoals" we fairly commenced our tour, though in the plan of this book the description of this place comes towards the end. But, before proceeding any farther, we wish to say something definite in favor of Maine.

Now we know that that which is dearly bought is highly prized; and hence scenes viewed when travelling afar are esteemed above those found nigh at hand. Tourists flock annually to the Old World in search of natural beauties, as if there were nothing in our own land to excite admiration. And yet we have every variety of mountain and coast scenery, equal, if not superior, to that of foreign countries, almost within sight of all our doors.

We hear much, for instance, of the coast-scenery of Cornwall, the Isle of Wight, and the Mediterranean, but still we do not fear to place in comparison the varied and romantic beauties of the coast of Maine. The entire seaboard is fretted and fringed in the most remarkable manner, forming a long-drawn labyrinth of capes, bays, headlands, and isles. The mingling of land and water is indeed admirable. Here a cape, clad in pine greenery, extends out into the sea, coquettishly encircling a great field of blue waves; there a bold headland, with its outlying drongs, meets and buffets the billows with catapultic force; here the bright fiord runs merrily up into the land, the hills stepping down to its borders, mirroring their outlines as in a glass; there a hundred isles are sown, like sparkling emeralds, in the summer sea.

We need not plunge into the wild interior of Maine, and wander amid its mountains and lakes and streams, in order to discover a wealth of beauty. All that one can reasonably desire is found on the border. Sailing northward, the shores of the Atlantic are found comparatively uninteresting until we approach the coast of Maine, when all tameness vanishes, and the shore puts on a bold, rugged beauty that could hardly be surpassed.

Whoever carefully examines a good map of the continents will perceive that, in a multitude of cases, amounting almost to a general rule, the capes point southward, and that groups of islands are found south of the land. Or otherwise, that, as we proceed southward, we find the land tapering away and terminating in islands. This we have seen is eminently true of the coast of Maine. To account for the present configuration of this coast is extremely difficult. It looks as if its shores had been broken and serrated by glaciers, which, as Agassiz tells us, once covered the entire State. Before the retreat of the ice period, those vast glaciers, slowly descending from the mountains to the sea, might perhaps, in long ages, have thus ploughed out portions of the shores, forming capes and bays; yet we must in many cases account, for the islands at least, by other causes. Some are clearly the result of upheaval, while others may have been formed by the sinking of neighboring land beneath the surface of the waves. Yet, however this may be, the coast of Maine presents an appearance similar to what the Duke of Bourbon called, " that nook-shotten isle of Albion." And from its broken outline comes its beauty.

And it will be the aim of the writer in the present work to do something like justice to this really remarkable region, which is one that in the course of time must be very widely known and thoroughly appreciated by that rapidly increasing class who delight in all the varied and wayward moods of Nature, so splendidly illustrated among the mountains and along the shores between the Isles of Shoals and Grand Menan.

As regards the accommodations for travel, comparatively little has been said, though they will be found quite ample. They are subject to more or less change from season to season, and are at the same time improving. New resorts are continually being found out, which necessitates new means of communication. For Mount Desert direct, the favorite route from Boston is by rail to Portland, and thence by steamer to Southwest and Bar Harbors: though such as have an unconquerable dread of the sea can proceed by rail to Bangor, and reach the island by the stage route. But thus they miss one great charm, namely, the ocean views of Mount Desert, which, to be thoroughly enjoyed, must be seen from every point of approach.

It should also be remembered that the steamer now runs regularly, in the season, from Portsmouth to the Isles of Shoals; while a similar swift and reliable convenience connects Eastport with Grand Menan, thus divesting the journey to that remarkable place of all the uncertainties and risks that in former times prevented so many from enjoying its attractions, now placed only a couple of hours, at the farthest, from the neighboring main. Railway guides will enable the tourist to count the cost.

For such as live to eat, and are curious about the matter of lodgings, there can be but little more than the general remark, that, both as regards quality and expense, the same variation is found on the New England coast that is characteristic of the city of New York. Slender consolations, indeed! At any moment the feast may be turned into a famine. It will be the business of Jenkins, who has fared sumptuously (and freely) at the one, to warn you, specially, of the other. After the elegant entertainments of Portland and Appledore (Isles of Shoals), the tourist will experience a steady decline; on the way down in the scale reaching the average at Mount Desert; and touching bottom with the necessarily frugal fare of Grand Menan. All, save epicures, will find the real feast everywhere spread out of doors, free of cost to every comer. It is this class for whom the author caters; and if they cannot rest satisfied during a summer vacation with what the following pages offer, they will do well by staying away from the New England coast altogether.

MOUNT DESERT.

CHAPTER II.

DEPARTURE FROM THE ISLES OF SHOALS — AGAMENTICUS — NIGHT — SUNRISE — BECALMED — THE VIEW OF MOUNT DESERT — ASHORE — THE MOUNTAINS.

ANDERING along the coast, we found ourselves, in course of time, at the Isles of Shoals, where we took passage in a trim-looking schooner for Mount Desert. We sailed in the morning with a fresh southerly breeze. It was not long before we had a fine view of Agamenticus, which rises to the height of several hundred feet, sending out its greeting from afar.

At this point, Mr. Oldstyle, the chief Historian of the party, and who is really to be held responsible for the most of what is said in the previous chapter, felt a slight attack of sea-sickness; yet his unfailing enthusiasm, united with the potent virtues of a lemon, kept him up, and he managed to relate many things about Agamenticus in the days of yore, and, among others, that this place was early designed to be a sort of metropolitan city. In 1642 Edward Godfrey was duly appointed the mayor, while the same authority provided for two fairs to be "held and kept" there "every year, forever thereafter" upon the Festivals of SS. James' and Paul's. The fate of this embryo city reminds us of the fact that the best laid plans of mice and men oft "gang agley." Nevertheless, Agamenticus forms a noble land-mark.

The Skipper here gave the coast a wide berth, and laid his course due north-east, shortly running down the land, though not before we had gained a glimpse of the distant peak of Mount Washington. The wind held fresh until sunset, and by nightfall the schooner was off Penobscot Bay, when the light-house on Mount Desert Rock opened its bright eye.

Our progress during the night was slow, but when morning dawned we were not far from the isle of our dreams. I was aroused from my slumbers by Old Sol himself, who, like some rude linkboy thrusting his torch in one's face, rose from the sea and sent a broad beam in through the little cabin window into my berth, hitting me squarely in the eye. Thereupon I resolved to rise. But Mr. Oldstyle, fully determined to have the first glimpse of the land, was ahead of me; and while I was pulling on my boots, disappeared up the companion-way in his smart, swallow-tailed coat, with a long spy-glass under his arm. Aureole, a young gentleman of our party, who, under the influence of Neptune, was very quiet the day before, followed him, having now got his "sea-legs" on; and before I could get on deck I heard him engaging in the following brief colloquy:

"What land's that, Skipper?"

"Mount Desert, I reckon," was the reply, putting the accent on the last syllable of "Desert."

"How far off?"

"Six or eight miles, ma' be."

"When are we going to get there?"

"Don't know."

Thereupon I thought it high time to inquire into the real state of affairs; and accordingly I hurried on deck, and found that there was a dead calm, the mainsail hanging perpendicularly from its gaff, our little craft appearing altogether

> "As idle as a painted ship
> Upon a painted ocean."

Yet it was a splendid morning; and, besides, there lay our enchanted isle, towering up out of the calm sea, veiled in a thin mist, and gilded all over with the golden glories of the rising sun.

In order to find a scene that will equal this, we must sail far away into the Pacific Sea. At a distance the island appears like a single mountain, of great height. green around its sides, and bare at the summit, which, on this occasion, gleamed upon us through the mist like a pinnacle of gold.

We sat long gazing upon this beautiful prospect, not even desiring to come nearer, lest the vision should be dispelled. Yet with the sun came a light breeze, and as it approached in the distance, rippling the surface of the still sea, the Skipper unlashed the helm, and stood ready to steer his craft into port. And when the breeze came, it barely swung out the schooner's boom, though at last we managed to get steerage-way, and sailed slowly, wing and wing, and with a sort of classic pomp, the gull wheeling and the porpoise diving, and both showing a sort of welcome by escorting us on our voyage.

In due time we entered the Harbor, went ashore, and found comfortable quarters.

After being duly refreshed, we turned to the *Gazetteer*, and found it stated that Mount Desert is an island lying off the coast of Maine, at a distance of one hundred and ten miles east of Portland, being connected with the main-land by a bridge. Mr. Oldstyle, after consulting his notes, said that it was seen by Champlain in 1605, who called it *Mons Desert*. It is anything but a desert. Champlain judged of its character by the mountain-peak, so prominent when viewed from a distance, and which Whittier calls the "Bald mountain's shrubless brow," and

> "The gray and thunder-smitten pile
> Which marks afar the Desert Isle."

This land is to be distinguished from Mount Desert Rock, which lies in the ocean, fifteen miles south of the island, affording just room enough for the light-house. Mount Desert *Rock* is alluded to by Whittier, and I give his description, because it is as good as a photograph. He writes:

> "And Desert Rock, abrupt and bare,
> Lifts its gray turret in the air —
> Seen from afar, like some stronghold,
> Built by the ocean kings of old."

This island contains about one hundred square miles. It is fourteen miles long, and, on an average, about seven wide, its longer axis lying nearly north and south. On the east side a tongue of the sea extends seven miles into the land, and is called Somes' Sound. On either side of the entrance to this Sound is a small harbor, one being called the North-east, and the other the South-west Harbor. Bar Harbor, where the steamer has a landing, is on the north-east side of the island. Here one of the Porcupine Islands is joined to Mount Desert by a sandy bar. Other islands are scattered around on every hand, adding greatly to the effect of the scenery.

But the mountains are the great distinguishing feature of the island. They are situated in its southern part, and form thirteen distinct peaks, which descend by gradual slopes towards the west, and end at the east, in most cases, with abrupt precipices, four of which look down upon glittering lakes, while a fifth reflects its image in the briny waters of Somes' Sound.

The highest peak is that of Green Mountain, upon which the officers of the Coast Survey built their observatory, and which served as the chief point in their complicated series of triangulations. The height of

this mountain is computed at fifteen hundred and
thirty-five feet above the level of the sea. These
mountains are the bones of the earth, which, being
broken and upheaved, form some of our most striking
and beautiful scenery, giving us lovely valleys, wild
mountain passes and sparkling fresh-water lakes, within
the sound of the murmuring sea. This leads to a remark on one feature of Mount Desert, which combines
the characteristics of seashore and inland, Newport
and the Catskills. I say the Catskills, and not the
White Mountains, because the great grandeur, and
often the sublimity of the latter, will not allow of a
comparison. Yet here we have the same *style*, if
not the same degree, of beauty. The White-Moun-
tain Notch is here represented, not unworthily, by the
celebrated Notch which is situated between Dry and
Newport Mountain, on the road from Bar Harbor
to Otter Creek. Wandering alone in the stillness of
this wild and romantic retreat, one can scarcely realize that he is indeed so near the shore of the loud-
sounding sea. Mrs. Browning's description of her
imaginary island applies with equal fitness to this,
when she writes:

"An island full of hills and dells,
　All rumpled and uneven
With green recesses, sudden swells,
　And odorous valleys, driven
So deep and straight, that always there
　The wind is cradled to soft air."

But all these features of Mount Desert, with its lakes and ponds and cliffs and trout-brooks and picturesque shores, will be described in detail elsewhere: so let us not anticipate the feast with a few crumbs.

A STORM BREWING — CONSULTATION — A VOTE FOR HISTORY — BIARD — A FALSE ALARM.

HAVING gained a general acquaintance with the place, posted ourselves with regard to the routes, and the best way of "doing" the island, an easterly storm came on, which promised to keep us indoors for a couple of days. A storm on the shore of Mount Desert affords many a fine sight, yet we did not come to see what Æolus could do in tossing breakers. Nevertheless, we accepted the situation, and when we found the gale rising, and the great raindrops dashing against the windows, we laid aside our canes and extemporized alpenstocks, and assembled in the little parlor for mutual counsel and advice.

And what should we do? Various propositions were made, but nothing seemed to meet the views of our party, which had been increased by the addition of three or four very pleasant and companionable persons, many of whom we always find here. Finally it was proposed to have a reading, and one suggested that it should be historic. The countenance of our antiquarian friend, Mr. Oldstyle, beamed with satisfaction at this, yet his expression quickly changed when Aureole, a youthful family connection, broke out, saying, "Yes, exactly, let 'us have Mr. Pickwick's monograph on the source of Hampstead Ponds." But Mr. Oldstyle met this exhibition of unseemly levity with such a severe frown, and looked so concerned for the dignity of history, that, while a young lady giggled, the rest of the company quite failed to see the point of the joke. Therefore our worthy friend improved the occasion to remind us of the wish expressed before leaving home, to read the account of the planting and destruction of the French colony of Mount Desert, on the ground, and amid the scenes where the events occurred. We therefore decided to have a Morning with the Jesuits. Mr. Oldstyle accordingly produced a roll of manuscript containing a translation of Father Biard's Narrative, as given in the first volume of the *Relations des Jesuites*, recently published at Quebec, "a better knowledge of which," said Mr. Oldstyle, as he looked up at us over his spectacles, " would have saved many writers on this subject from serious blunders."

It is a notable fact that this subject has often been treated with perfect recklessness. Bancroft states in the earlier editions of his History that the French Colony of St. Savior was established on the "north bank of the Penobscot," while his last revision puts it on the *east side* of the Isle of Mount Desert.

The *date* of this attempt at colonization by the French has seldom been stated with any accuracy, while in regard to the period of time spent by the French on the island few seem to have known anything at all. Some observations to this effect were made, and attention was called to the fact that the old inhabitants of the isle were reckless on this point. Whereupon Aureole confidently offered the opinion that history was "all bosh, any way."

Mr. Oldstyle received this remark of his young relative with silent indignation; yet, while proceeding to unroll his manuscript, he took occasion to confess that history, and especially American history, was often pursued in a spirit productive of little real good, the truth being too often held subservient to popular tradition.

Mr. Oldstyle, though somewhat advanced in years, evidently leaned toward the new school of history, now springing up, which is devoted to the elucidation of Truth, without any reference to its cost. He did not, however, think it worth while to enter upon a discussion of these points; and, accordingly, after briefly stating the reasons which led the French colonists to establish themselves on the coast of Maine, in 1613, he began as follows:

Father Biard's Relation.

"We were detained five days at Port Royal, by adverse winds, when a favorable north-easter having arisen, we set out with the intention of sailing up Pentegoët [Penobscot] River, to a place called Kadesquit, which had been allotted for our new residence, and which possessed great advantages for this purpose. But God willed otherwise, for when we had reached the south-eastern coast of the Island of Menan, the weather changed, and the sea was covered with a fog so dense that we could not distinguish day from night. We were greatly alarmed, for this place is full of breakers and rocks, upon which, in the darkness, we feared our vessel might drift. The wind not permitting us to put out to sea, we remained in this position two days and two nights, veering sometimes to one side, sometimes to another, as God inspired us. Our tribulation led us to pray to God to deliver us from danger, and send us to some place where we might contribute to His glory. He heard us, in His mercy, for on the same evening we began to discover the stars, and in the morning the fog had cleared away. We then discovered that we were near the coast of Mount Desert, an island which the savages call Pemetic. The pilot steered towards the eastern shore, and landed us in a large and beautiful harbor. We returned thanks to God, elevating the Cross, and singing praises with the holy Sacrifice of the Mass. We named the place and harbor St. Savior."

A Rainy Morning with the Jesuits.

This harbor, Mr. Oldstyle thought, was North-east Harbor, though, in the absence of authorities, he would not be too positive. He then continued:

"Now in this port of St. Savior a violent quarrel arose between our sailors and crew and the other passengers. The cause of it was that the charter granted, and the agreement made in France, was to the effect that the said sailors should be bound to put into any port in Acadia that we should designate, and should remain there three months. The sailors maintained that they had arrived in a port in Acadia, and that the said term of three months ought to date from this arrival. To this it was answered that this port was not the one designated, which was Kadesquit, and therefore that the time they were in St. Savior was not to be taken into account. The pilot held obstinately to a contrary opinion, maintaining that no vessel had ever landed at Kadesquit, and that he did not wish to become a discoverer of new routes. There was much argument for and against these views, discussions were being carried on incessantly, a bad omen for the future.

"While this question was pending," says the Father, "the Savages made a fire, in order that we might see the smoke. This signal meant that they had observed us, and wished to know if we needed them, which we did. The pilot took the opportunity to tell them that the Fathers from Port Royal were in his ship. The Savages replied that they would be very glad to see one whom they had known at Pentegoët two years before. This was Father Biard, who went immediately to see them, and inquired the route to Kadesquit, informing them that he intended to reside there. 'But,' said they, 'if you desire to remain there, why do you not remain instead with us, who have as good a place as Kadesquit is?' They then began to praise their settlement, assuring him that it was so healthy and so pleasant, that when the natives were sick anywhere else they were brought there and were cured. These eulogies did not greatly impress Father Biard, because he knew sufficiently well that the Savages, like other people, overrated, sometimes, their own possessions. Nevertheless, they understood how to induce him to remain, for they said: 'You must come, for our Sagamore Asticou is dangerously ill, and if you do not come, he will die without baptism, and will not go to heaven, and you will be the cause of it, for he wishes to be baptized.' The reason, so naturally given, made Father Biard hesitate, and they finally persuaded him to go, since he had but three leagues to travel, and there would be no greater loss of time than a single afternoon."

Here the reader paused to tell us that one edition of Biard says that this spot was separated from the island of Mount Desert, which, by the French, was supposed to include only the land lying east of Somes' Sound. He then continued:

"We embarked in their canoe with Sieur de la Motte, and Simon. the Interpreter, and we set out.

"When we arrived at Asticou's wigwam, we found him ill, but not dangerously so, for he was only suffering from rheumatism; and finding this, we decided to pay a visit to the place which the Indians had boasted was so much better than Kadesquit for the residence of Frenchmen. We found that the Savages had in reality reasonable grounds for their eulogies. We felt very well satisfied with it ourselves, and, having brought these tidings to the remainder of the crew, it was unanimously agreed that we should remain there, and not seek further, seeing that God himself seemed to intend it, by the train of happy accidents that had occurred, and by the miraculous cure of a child, which I shall relate elsewhere.

"This place is a beautiful hill, sloping gently from the sea-shore, and supplied with water by a spring on each side. The ground comprises from twenty-five to thirty acres, covered with grass, which, in some places, reaches the height of a man. It fronts the south and east, towards Pentegoët Bay, into which are discharged the waters of several pretty streams, abounding in fish. The soil is rich and fertile. The port and harbor are the finest possible, in a position commanding the entire coast; the harbor especially is smooth as a pond, being shut in by the large island of Mount Desert, besides being surrounded by certain small islands which break the force of the winds and waves, and fortify the entrance. It is large enough to hold any fleet, and is navigable for the largest ships up to a cable's length from the shore. It is in latitude forty-four and one-half degrees north, a position more northerly than that of Bordeaux."

Mr. Oldstyle here also gave as his opinion that the place finally fixed upon as the site for their new habitation was located on the western side of Somes' Sound, on the farm of Mr. Fernald. The reader then went on:

"When we had landed in this place, and planted the Cross, we began to work, and with the work began our disputes, the omen and origin of our misfortunes. The cause of these disputes was that our Captain, La Saussaye, wished to attend to agriculture, and our other leaders besought him not to occupy the workmen in that manner, and so delay the erection of dwellings and fortifications.[1] He would not comply with their request, and from these disputes arose others, which lasted until the English obliged us to make peace in the manner I am about to relate."

Mr. Oldstyle omitted Biard's statement of the position of the English in America, in which he declares that the distance intervening between their colony and those of the French rendered all quarreling needless. Continuing:

"The English colonists in Virginia are in the habit of coming every year to the islands of Pencoit, twen-

---

(1) Here Father Biard leaves it undecided whether any fortifications were put up; but Charlevoix says that they "hastily threw up a slight entrenchment."

A Rainy Morning with the Jesuits. 31

ty-five leagues from St. Savior, in order to provide food [fish] for the winter. While on their way, as usual, in the summer of the year 1613, they were overtaken out at sea by fogs and mists, which in this region often overspread both land and sea, in summer. These lasted some days, during which the tide drifted them gradually farther than they intended. They were about eighty leagues farther in New France than they supposed, but they did not recognize the place."

Here our excellent friend, who never hesitated to call a spade a spade, explained to us that this was the ship of Samuel Argall, ostensibly a trader, but practically a pirate, like a large number of men of his class, who, in those early times, roved the seas. He had sailed the previous May for the Isles of Shoals, to catch codfish, in a vessel carrying fourteen guns and sixty men, and now he had lost his reckoning in the fog, and improved the occasion to murder and plunder the French. In his letter to Nicholas Hawes, said Mr. Oldstyle, sarcastically, he speaks of his *fishing* voyage, in which he beseeches "God of his mercy to bless us." Aureole put in the remark, that "He was doubtless as respectable a man as a good many others never found out;" which remark, though felt, was ignored, as Mr. Oldstyle was somewhat averse to the encouragement of such unsettling opinions among the young. Failing in this, the festive Aureole, who had been sitting astride his chair, with his chin resting upon the top bar, looking out of the window, now fancied he saw a ship running into the harbor, through the driving rain and fog. He consequently interrupted the reading by calling the company to view this unexpected visitor, while Mr. Oldstyle laid aside his spectacles, and aimed mine host's spy-glass toward the point indicated by Aureole. But nothing could be seen, while Aureole himself suggested that it was the Flying Dutchman. Mr. Oldstyle, however, suspected that it was simply a ruse to break up the reading, which Aureole viewed as a sort of bore. Nevertheless, we all took our seats again, except Aureole, who went to look into the condition of his fishing-tackle, while Mr. Oldstyle benignantly put on his spectacles to resume the story. But the remainder must be reserved for the next chapter.

A RAINY MORNING WITH THE JESUITS.
[CONTINUED.]

CHAPTER IV.

ARGALL APPEARS — THE FIGHT — THE SURRENDER — DEATH OF DU THET — THE FATE OF THE FRENCH — ARGALL'S DEPARTURE AND RETURN — BIARD.

ILENCE once more prevailed in our little circle, though the storm continued without, and as we glanced across South-west Harbor, we saw that

"Thro' scudding drifts the rainy Hyades
Vext the dim sea."

Accordingly Mr. Oldstyle resumed the story, as follows:

"Some Savages observed their vessel and went to meet them, supposing them to be Frenchmen in search of them. The English understood nothing of what the Savages said, but conjectured from their signs that there was a vessel near, and that this vessel was French. They understood the word 'Normans,' which the Savages called us, and in the polite gestures of the natives, they recognized the French ceremonies of courtesy. Then the English, who were in need of provisions, and of every thing else, ragged, half naked, and in search of plunder, inquired carefully how large our vessel was, how many canoes we had, how many men, etc., and having received a satisfactory answer, uttered cries of joy, demonstrating that they had found what they wanted, and that they intended to attack us. The Savages did not interpret it so, however, for they supposed the English to be our friends, who desired earnestly so see us. Accordingly one of them guided the English to our vessel. As soon as the English saw us they began to prepare for combat, and their guide then saw that he had made a mistake, and began to weep and curse those who had deceived him. Many times afterwards he wept and implored pardon for his error of us, and of the other Savages, because they wished to avenge our misfortunes on him, believing that he had acted through malice.

"On seeing this vessel approach us, we knew not whether we were to see friends or enemies, Frenchmen or foreigners. The pilot therefore went forward in a sloop to reconnoitre, while the rest were arming themselves. La Saussaye remained ashore, and with him the greater number of the men. Lieutenant La Motte, Ensign Ronfere, Sergeant Joubert, and the rest went on board the ship.

"The English vessel moved quickly as an arrow, having the wind astern. It was hung at the waist with red, the arms of England floated over it, and three trumpets and two drums were ready to sound. Our pilot, who had gone forward to reconnoitre, did not return to the ship, fearing, as he said, to fall into their hands, to avoid which, he rowed himself around an island. Thus the ship did not contain one-half its crew, and was defended only by ten men, of whom but one, Captain Flory, had had any experience in naval contests. Although not wanting in prudence or courage, the Captain had not time to prepare for a conflict, nor had his crew; there was not even time to weigh anchor, so as to disengage the ship, which is the first step to be taken in sea fights. It would, however, have been of little use to weigh the anchor, since the sails were fastened; for, being summer, they had arranged them as an awning to shade the decks. This mishap, however, had a good result, for our men being sheltered during the combat, and the English unable to take aim at them, fewer of them were killed or wounded.

"As soon as they approached, our sailors hailed them, but the English replied only by cries of menace, and by discharges of musketry and cannon. They had fourteen pieces of artillery and sixty artillerymen, who ranged themselves along the side of their vessel, firing rapidly, without taking aim. The first discharge was terrible; the whole ship was shrouded in fire and smoke. On our side the guns remained silent. Captain Flory cried out, 'Put the cannon in position,' but the gunner was absent. Father Gilbert du Thet, who had never been guilty of cowardice in his life, hearing the Captain's order, and seeing that no one obeyed, took the match and fired the cannon as loudly as the enemy's. The misfortune was that he did not aim carefully; had he done so, probably something more useful than noise would have occurred.

"The English, after their first attack, prepared to board our vessel. Captain Flory cut the cable, and thus arrested for a time the progress of the enemy. They then prepared to fire another volley, and in this du Thet was wounded by a musket, and fell across the helm. Captain Flory and three other men were also wounded, and they cried out that they surrendered. The English, on hearing this cry, went into their boat to board our vessel, our men imprudently rushed into theirs in order to put off to shore before the arrival of the victors. The conquerors cried out to them to return, as otherwise they would fire on them, and two of our men, in their terror, threw themselves into the water and were drowned, either because they were wounded or, more probably, were shot while in the water. They were both promising young men, one named Le Moine, from Dieppe, and the other named Nenen, from Beauvais. Their bodies were found nine days afterwards, and carefully interred. Such was the history of the capture of our vessel."

Here the Honorary Member inquired if Mr. Bancroft did not say in his notice of the event that the

English bombarded the French fort. Mr. Oldstyle replied that he *did*, but that his statement lacked *authority;* for himself, he would not take anything without "authority."

"Just so," said the Honorary Member; while the Reader went on to recite, not wholly without indignation, the story of Argall's perfidy:

"The victorious Englishmen made a landing in the place where we had begun to erect our tents and dwellings, and searched our Captain to find his commission, saying that the land was theirs, but that if we would show that we had acted in good faith, and under the authority of our Prince, they would not drive us away, since they did not wish to imperil the amicable relations between our two Sovereigns. The trouble was that they did not find La Saussaye, but they seized his desk, searched it carefully, and having found our commissions and royal letters, seized them, then putting everything in its place, they closed and locked the desk. On the next day, when he saw La Saussaye, the English Captain welcomed him politely, and then asked to see his commission. La Saussaye replied that his papers were in his desk, which was accordingly brought to him, and he found that it was locked and in perfect order, but that the papers were missing. The English captain immediately changed his tone and manner, saying, 'Then, sir, you are imposing on us. You give us to understand that you hold a commission from your King, and yet you can produce no evidence of if. You are all rogues and pirates, and deserve death.' He then granted permission to his soldiers to plunder us, in which work they spent the entire afternoon. We witnessed the destruction of our property from the shore, the Englishmen having fastened our vessels to theirs, for we had two, our ship and a boat newly constructed and equipped. We were thus reduced to a miserable condition, and this was not all. Next day they landed and robbed us of all we still possessed, destroying also our clothing and other things. At one time they committed some personal violence on two of our people, which so enraged them that they fled into the woods, like poor crazed creatures, half naked, and without any food, not knowing what was to become of them."

We now come, said Mr. Oldstyle, to learn the fate of the brave ecclesiastic, who, while professional soldiers fled, had the courage to stand by the guns:

"To return to the Jesuits: I have told you that Father du Thet was wounded by a musket-shot during the fight. The English, on entering our ship, placed him under the care of their surgeon, along with the other wounded men. This surgeon was a Catholic, and a very charitable man, and he treated us with great kindness. Father Biard, knowing that Father du Thet was wounded, asked the Captain to allow him to be carried ashore, so that he had an opportunity to receive the last Sacraments, and to praise the just and merciful God, in company with his brethren. He died with much resignation, calmness, and devotion, twenty-four hours after he was wounded. Thus his prayers were granted, for, on our departure from Honfleur, he had raised his hands and eyes toward heaven, praying that he might return no more to France, but that he might die laboring for the salvation of souls, and especially of the Savages. He was buried the same day at the foot of a large cross which we had erected on our arrival.

"It was not till then that the English recognized the Jesuits to be priests. Father Biard and Father Ennemond Masse went to the ship to speak to the English captain, and explained frankly to him that they were Jesuits, who had travelled into these regions to convert the Savages. Then they implored him, by the blood of Him whom they both acknowledged as their Redeemer, and by the mercy they hoped for, that he would have pity on the poor Frenchmen, whom God had placed in his power, that he would liberate them, and permit them to return to France. The Captain heard them quietly, and answered them respectfully. 'But,' said he, 'I wonder that you Jesuits, who are generally supposed to be conscientious and religious men, should be here in company with robbers and pirates, people without law or religion.'

"Father Biard replied to him, proving that all the crew were good men, and approved by his Most Christian Majesty, and refuted so positively the objections of the English captain, that the latter was obliged to pretend to be convinced. 'Certainly,' said he, 'it was very wrong to lose your letters patent. However, I shall talk with your captain about sending you home.' And from that time, he made the two Fathers share his table, showing them much kindness and respect. But one thing annoyed him greatly, the escape of the pilot and sailors, of whom he could hear nothing. The pilot was a native of Rouen, named Le Pailleur; he had gone away to reconnoitre, as I have already mentioned, and being unable to return to the ship in time, he stayed apart in his sloop, and when night fell, took with him the other sailors, and placed himself in security from the power of the English. At night he came to advise with us as to what he had better do. He did this to oblige the Jesuits, for he came to Father Biard, and taking his hand, begged him not to distrust him, assuring him that he would be faithful to him and the other Fathers. As he seemed to speak sincerely, Father Biard thanked him affectionately, and promised to remember his kindness. The Father also said that he would not think of himself until the others had set out, that then he would seek counsel of God; and he warned the pilot not to fall into the hands of the English, because the captain was very anxious to catch him. The pilot profited by the warning, for in two or three days after, he retired behind some of the islands, to be in shelter, and to watch for what might happen. The English captain then resolved not to inflict any further injury on us, although he might have desired to do so, as I conjectured by his previous conduct. He was a very able and artful man, but nevertheless a gentleman and a man of courage. His crew were neither cruel or unkind to any of us."

The narrative was concluded as follows: "It is difficult to believe how much sorrow we experienced during this time, for we did not know what was to be our fate. On the one hand, we expected either death or slavery from the English; and on the other, to remain in this country and live an entire year among the Savages, seemed to us a lingering and painful death. The Savages, having heard of our disasters, came to us and offered to do all in their power for us, promising to feed us during the winter, and showing us great kindness. But we could not see any hope before us, and we did not know how we could live in such a desert."

Mr. Oldstyle then told us, in brief, how a way was opened for their disposition by this man whom the Jesuit, who was soured against the French leaders, curiously praises as a gentleman. La Saussaye, Father Masse, and thirteen others were mercilessly cast off in an open boat, instead of being put on board a French vessel, as Bancroft says. This company, when joined among the islands by the pilot and his boat, who fled previous to the fight, made their way eastward by the aid of oars, coasting chiefly along the shore until, on the southern coast of Nova Scotia, they found two trading-vessels, in which they secured a passage to St. Malo. On the other hand, Father Biard and thirteen of the company were carried prisoners to Virginia, where Sir Thomas Dale, Governor of Virginia, threatened them with the halter, so that Argall was finally obliged to confess that he had stolen the commission of La Saussaye from his desk at Mount Desert. This theft was perpetrated to justify his own piracy, for which he richly deserved to suffer the penalty of the law, as the two nations were then at peace, and no excuse whatever could be urged for this cruel deed. Yet, said the narrator, they were not even satisfied with the wrong and mischief that they had actually done, and Argall soon fitted out his own ship and the captured vessel of La Saussaye, together with a third smaller vessel, for the purpose of destroying Port Royal. In this expedition they were accompanied by Father Biard, who, according to certain English and French writers, encouraged the attack "out of indigestible malice" (Purchas, Vol. iv. 1808,) which he had conceived against his old enemy, Biencourt, then in charge at that place. Biard himself gives the contrary impression, yet he allows that both the French and English looked upon him as a traitor; and, while the English desired to hang him, one of the French ended a parley with him at Port Royal by saying, "Begone, or I will split your head with this hatchet." Mr. Oldstyle thought that the Jesuit's character needed looking into; yet he went on to tell us how Argall sailed the second time for St. Savior, expecting to find that another ship had arrived from France, being still bent on plunder. But he met no one except peaceful Indians. Landing at this beautiful place, the English destroyed everything that remained. Says Father Biard, "They burnt our fortifications and pulled down our crosses, and put up one as a sign that they were taking possession of the land as Lords. This cross had the name of the King of Great Britain engraved upon it."

Argall continued here some time, long enough indeed for one of his men to attempt a conspiracy against him, and thus these thieves fell out among themselves. Yet the plan failed, and Father Biard writes that " they also hanged one of their men for a conspiracy in the same place where eight days before they had taken down the first of our crosses."

This ended Mr. Oldstyle's story, for which we all felt greatly obliged, the feeling of the party culminating in a vote of thanks.

The Colony of St. Savior therefore perished. For this high-handed outrage the French, owing to the disturbed condition of European politics, were unable to obtain proper indemnification. Madame de Guercheville only succeeded in recovering La Saussaye's ship.

As it may be interesting to the reader to learn the fate of Father Biard, we may relate here that Argall's fleet, on its return to Virginia from the destruction of Port Royal, was overtaken by a gale, in which one vessel was lost, while that in which the Jesuit sailed was driven to the Azores. The Commander, Lieutenant Turnel, afterwards decided to sail to Pembroke, in Wales, where Father Biard was set ashore, being well received by the Protestant Ecclesiastics. From thence he went to France, where, as a theological Professor, he perhaps found more quiet employment for a time, though he ended his days as a chaplain in the army.

SOMES' SOUND.

CHAPTER V.

SOUTH-WEST HARBOR — FIRST IMPRESSIONS — THE SOUND — THE SCENERY — FERNALD'S POINT — THE FRENCH — BIARD'S SPRING — DOG MOUNTAIN — MONEY DIGGERS.

SUMMER tourists who enter Mount Desert by the way of South-west Harbor are liable to receive very unfavorable impressions of this beautiful island. While approaching the shore, the most charming views are obtained, but after the first salutation their majesties the mountains become shy, and when the steamer reaches the pier they are wholly lost to sight. On landing, an ancient, fish-like smell is found to pervade the air around the dock in the vicinity of the lobster-boiling establishment, while the general aspect of the place is hardly inviting. By crossing the harbor to the Ocean House, the view of the mountains may indeed be regained, yet the prospect from the east side is tame.

Still no one should feel discouraged, since many of the chief attractions of Mount Desert are situated within a short distance of the village, where the visitor, if he is wise, will spend at least a third of the time allotted to his sojourn on the island. One of the loveliest places thus accessible is "Somes' Sound," a body of water, six or seven miles long, formed by an arm of the sea, which nearly divides the island in the middle. Admirable views of the sound may be enjoyed by a walk of five or ten minutes from the hotels to the east side of Clark's Point, where is found a rocky shore well suited to summer idling. Yet the best way to explore this part of the island is to take a boat and sail leisurely up to Somesville. It is the custom to start from South-west Harbor, and, rounding Clark's Point, to steer for Fernald's Point. The scenery thus appears to the best advantage. As we proceed, the sound, which is about two miles wide at the entrance, assumes the character of a noble river, fenced in by rugged mountains and fair green hills, the margin being diversified by points and coves. From a distance, looking up the sound, the view resembles that of the Delaware Water Gap, while on a nearer approach it forcibly brings to mind the Hudson at the Highlands. But here, however, there are no unsightly works of man to mar the prospect. An occasional cottage may be seen nestling among the hills, and the fishing-smack is found at anchor, the crew busily engaged in setting their nets, but otherwise nature appears in all her untamed wildness.

The entrance to the sound is shut in by islands, so that we do not realize our nearness to the sea; yet here, under the shadow of the hills, where we are often reminded of Lake George, the fisher-boy hauls up the portly cod and the haddock, while anon the whole surface ripples with schools of herring and menhaden.

The sound cuts through the centre of the mountain-range at right angles between Dog Mountain and Mount Mansell, which name we gave to the elevation on the eastern side, partly because it has heretofore had no recognized name, but more especially for the reason that at an early period the whole island was so called by the English, in honor of Sir Robert Mansell. This mountain is of no considerable height, yet it lends great beauty to the prospect, its summit being more or less bare. Dog Mountain, however, attains a fine elevation, and reflects its perpendicular face in the deep waters that sparkle around its feet. Through the splendid gateway formed by these two mountains, we pass into the broader waters beyond, and gain a glimpse of the pastoral scenery which is found around Somesville.

Within the protecting reaches of Somes' Sound, the French decided to establish their new home. We have already seen that the precise spot was at what is now known as Fernald's Point. Towards this place we laid our course with no little interest the first time we were out boating, after the recital of Father Biard's Narrative when storm-bound at the inn. It was a charming day, and nearly the entire mountain-range could be clearly distinguished, though the eastern sections were the most prominent, Green Mountain lifting itself above all the rest, crowned by the little public house which marks its top. A pleasant breeze soon carried us on to Fernald's Point, a beautiful grassy piece of land which sweeps gently up from the shore, precisely as Father Biard describes it, terminating in a small but finely formed ridge of naked rock. Landing here, we walked over the ground, which includes very nearly the precise number of acres indicated by the Relation, and which are characterized by a rich and fertile soil. Here we looked down upon the harbor, "smooth as a pond," with the bold water navigable for the largest ships, " up to within a cable's length of the shore," and the entrance strongly fortified against wind and weather by rockbound yet sunny isles.

The account says that the place where the French settled, was "shut in by the large island of Mount Desert," a statement that appears to have misled some persons. The explanation was briefly given in a previous chapter, where the reader was informed that the French supposed the land on the west side of the sound to be wholly separated from that on the east, which, on account of the barren aspect of the mountains, they called Mount Desert. And now here lay before us the same old mountains of which the priest wrote. Mr. Oldstyle was charmed with the exactness of the description, which he rightly declared to be photographic, and incapable of application to any other spot on the coast of Maine.

While at the farm-house, we inquired if there were any springs of water on the Point, as ·Biard says that it "was supplied with water by a spring on each side." The query was promptly answered by Mr. Fernald, who led us to a spring on the east side, and one also on the west. That on the east side ran into the sound. Its outlet has been greatly disturbed by the wearing away of the shore, yet we found the water still running. That on the west side of the Point overflows into a little cove, boiling up out of the sand with considerable force. At high tide the salt water flows into it, yet when the tide recedes the spring is found as pure and fresh as before. This spring was running here when the ancestors of the Fernalds first settled on the land, and is beyond question the identical spring at which the Jesuit Fathers quenched their thirst in the summer of 1613. The water is cold and inexhaustible, fishing-fleets often coming here in dry season, when the wells fail, to fill their tanks and casks.

Of French relics there are none. The shell-heaps seen near the shore must be referred to the Indians, who evidently dwelt upon this sightly place. The graves of the French killed in the fight with Argall have never been discovered. Father Vetromile, in his work on the Abenakis Indians, indeed gives a picture purporting to represent the grave of du Thet, yet the sketch is a pure fancy, designed perhaps to impress the imagination of the faithful. At an early period every vestige of the French completely passed away. Back of Flying Mountain, and directly under Eagle Cliff, in Dog Mountain, we were shown trenches, recently opened in connection with holes in the ground, having the appearance of ancient cellars. Our friend Aureole, who went with us, made light of these "cellars," while Mr. Oldstyle demonstrated that they were formed, like many others which he afterward showed in the woods, by the upturning of large trees. The parties who opened these trenches gave us the impression that they were laboring in the interests of history, yet our own view is that they were influenced by the mania for money-digging, of which something is to be said by and by. They evidently hoped to find treasure buried by the French.

We left the place and returned to the Point, which ought to be known as St. Savior, since the French evidently transferred the name given to their first landing-place to this; and, after drinking once more from the sparkling water of Father Biard's Spring, we embarked and sailed past Flying Mountain, landing upon the shore of the cove, not far from our friend's "cellars." Here a wrecked fishing-smack lay, quietly going to pieces. The place is one of very great beauty, being hemmed in on the west by Eagle Cliff, which rises to a height of eight or nine hundred feet.

Near this cliff is another, in the face of the same mountain. It looks down upon the deep water of the sound, which is navigable for large vessels up to its very base. It is altogether the most wonderful cliff on the island, the granite faces, nearly a thousand feet high, being inaccessible to mortals. We brought our boat under this dreadful precipice, where we could look up squarely into the crags. The view is sublime, but the position was one in which we did not care to linger, as in many places detached rocks of immense size seemed on the point of falling down. At the foot of the precipice lay vast quantities of *debris*, and we therefore gave the cliff a wide berth, sailing past to a point which made out into the sound. Here we landed, and discovered a place where it was possible to ascend the mountain. The course taken was well nigh perpendicular, and I was left to climb alone from rock to rock, hauling myself up by the stunted trees and shrubs, no one else caring to undergo the labor.

Finally I reached the top, and walked along the escarpment until I came to the edge of the perpendicular cliff. Here, looking down, the scene was most impressive. The boat, with her white sail, now seemed scarcely larger than a gull, while our party, who had climbed up a short distance from the water and perched themselves upon a jutting rock to await the result of my adventure, were now reduced to pigmies. I shouted aloud to Amarinta, but could not make myself understood. I waved my hat, but was not observed. I at last found that I must take a position on the highest peak, where my figure would stand out sharply defined against the sky. Here I was soon seen, and to my signal Amarinta's dainty pocket-handkerchief fluttered a reply. Then in response to my loud halloo, came a small voice. The cambric waved again, and I caught two syllables that floated slowly up from the depths below,—*Take care!* It was the small voice which belonged to the anxious proprietor of the pocket-handkerchief. As for Oldstyle, he viewed me through his glass with as much unconcern as though I had been an eagle or a crow; while Aureole lay prone upon the rock in utter idleness, thus saving the polish of his patent-leather boots.

All along the edge of the cliff the bare granite is full of horrid seams and rifts, while huge sections seem ready at any minute to plunge downward into the sound below. A hint from a handful of gunpowder would dislodge millions of tons. Here I was most forcibly reminded of Shakspeare's description of Dover Cliffs in King Lear, which applies to these, with the exception of the samphire-gatherer:

"Come on, Sir; here's the place:—stand still.—How fearful
And dizzy 'tis to cast one's eyes so low!
The crows, and choughs, that wing the midway air,
Show scarce so gross as beetles: half way down
Hangs one that gathers samphire; dreadful trade!
Methinks, he seems no bigger than his head:
The fishermen, that walk upon the beach,
Appear like mice; and yon, tall, anchoring bark,
Diminish'd to her cock; her cock, a buoy
Almost too small for sight: the murmuring surge
That on the unnumber'd idle pebbles chafes,
Cannot be heard so high."

Virgil says that the descent to Avernus is easy, yet the descent of this Cliff is twice as hard as the ascent, and requires double the time. It is finally accomplished, however, and after various slips and slides I reached the rock where our boat was moored, when we sailed out from under these frowning heights, which gradually sink towards the north, forming a valley, and then rise again pushing out into the sound. This valley, which terminates on the sound, is elevated only about forty or fifty feet above the water. The bank is of shelving granite, down which pours a small stream known as Man-of-War Brook, so called, tradition tells us, from the fact that in the last war with England the King's cruisers sailing along the coast were accustomed to put in here to fill their tanks. It certainly must have proved a convenient place for this purpose. As we sat in the boat, rocking gently upon the salt waves, our cups received the cool sparkling water of the brook—a child of the uplands —which even at this dry season was pouring down a bountiful supply. It was here very pleasing to notice the confidence of a pretty linnet, who alighted to share with us the benefit of the brook, perching herself on the point of a rock under the spray, and performing her ablutions with all the nice airs of a high-bred city bird.

On one side of the brook was a landing, and a couple of wild, amphibious looking boys were pushing out in a weather-beaten boat with an old black sail to go after haddock. Their trade had early put its seal upon them. O flesh, how fishified! Two little girls, with bare heads and feet, sat on the bank staring at us with beautiful dark brown eyes. Their features were good, but when we spoke to them it was mournful to hear the elder, about ten years old, answer in a hoarse voice, which clearly implied much physical neglect. The sun was broiling hot, and we asked if she had no bonnet, being told in reply that she had one last summer. She had no shoes, and last winter she froze her feet. Their parents lived in a log-house up in the valley. Having heard that there were money-diggers in the neighborhood, we inquired for the place where they were at work. The girls pointed up the valley and led the way. A short walk brought us to a wild and romantic spot where the ground had been partially cleared, and where granite cliffs, sprinkled with shaggy fir and spruce, rose up on the north side to a height of three or four hundred feet. In the middle of the cleared ground was an excavation large enough for the cellar of a good-sized house. The excavation extended down to the solid rock, which everywhere underlies the drift, and a couple of strange-looking men were hard at work with long-handled spades throwing out the earth. These were the money-diggers, whose faith was soon to be rewarded with untold treasures of silver and gold.

The history of money-digging in Maine is somewhat curious. There has scarcely ever been a time when the subject did not attract attention. Kendall, in his Travels, gives an account of a great sensation created in connection with the subject in the beginning of the present century, at Norridgewock, where a man and his two sons gave out that they had found immense treasures, and, on the strength of the representation, swindled the community out of a large amount of property. At that time a person was going about in the interior lecturing on the subject of hidden treasure, and exciting the imagination of the people.

From time to time money has actually been found. Not long since a pot of gold and a signet-ring were discovered on Richmond Island, near Portland, by a farmer, Mr. Hanscom, when ploughing. Four hundred dollars in French crowns were found in a field near Frenchman's Bay. Near Castine a large collection of old coins was found by Captain Stephen Grindle in the year 1840-1. The place pointed out is on the bank of the Bagaduce, six miles from the site of the fort. At this point, perhaps, was the old road to Mount Desert.

About the close of November, 1840, Captain Grindle was engaged with his son, hauling wood down to the shore, when the latter picked up a piece of money near a partially buried rock, lying about seventy-five feet from the shore, and in the old line of a beaten track that had existed for time out of mind. Tradition likewise says that one of the Indian routes from the peninsula of Castine to Mount Desert and Frenchman's Bay was up the Bagaduce, and thence across to Blue-Hill Bay.

The coin found was a French piece. This prize led them to commence digging in the ground, which they continued doing until dark, the search being rewarded by nearly twenty additional coins. During the night the snow fell, and nothing more was done until spring, when two coins were found embedded in the top of the rock. An iron bar thrust into the opening revealed the presence of a large quantity, numbering nearly five hundred pieces of different nations. Mr. Grindle's wife gleefully held her apron, which was soon loaded by her husband and son, she at the same time declaring that it was "the best lapful she had ever carried."

These may have been lost or hidden by Baron Castine, when, in 1688, he fled to the woods to escape from Governor Andross. One of the silver coins was recently shown me at Somesville by the person who received it from the finder.

Still nearer this spot, on the east side of the sound, opposite Fernald's Point, money has also been found. At least such is the common belief, which is based on good evidence. The reputed finder still lives (1868) on the place, where, according to the testimony of a man once in his employ, he discovered a pot of gold. At all events his circumstances appear to have suddenly changed, when he rose from a condition of hardship to one of comparative affluence and ease. That gold may have been buried there is not at all unlikely. When Argall attacked St. Savior, a part of the French were scattered in the woods and among the neighboring islands, and gold may have been buried by them at the place in question and never recovered.

All these circumstances, taken together, lead the somewhat credulous farmers and fishermen to imagine that gold is everywhere buried on their lands. This suspicion is strengthened by Spiritualists and Divining-rod men, who go from place to place, practicing upon the unsophisticated. We found one of the Spiritualists here in this valley. He was a man of somewhat good features with gray beard and hair, and a wild light in his eye. The diggers at first gave us the impression that they were making a cellar, but gradually the owner of the ground, a red-faced man, half farmer and half fisherman, unfolded the tremendous secret. Mr. Oldstyle and the rest did not enjoy his confidence, and it was reserved for my own ear to enjoy the revelation in full.

Drawing me aside, he began by requesting my opinion on the general subject of gold, and desired to know if the rock was gold-bearing, and whether, in case treasure was found, the United-States Government could take it away. I assured him that the rocks of Mount Desert were not auriferous, and that it was folly to look for treasure; moreover, that I thought, so far as the Government might be concerned,

he would be welcome to all that he could find. My
unbelief caused him to warm up, and to declare in a
low tone approaching a stage-whisper, "There's gold
here." This did not produce the startling effect
anticipated, and therefore, with a sort of insanity blaz-
ing from his eyes, he went on to unfold his belief.
He had signified in the beginning that the object in
view was a cellar, because he did not know who I was.
I might have been a spy, or the agent of some party
about to make a midnight raid upon the diggings.
But now that he felt assured he was dealing with an
honest tourist, he had no objection to telling me that
they were in search of gold, and that in three days
they would reach it. All the predictions made thus
far by the Spirits had been verified. They had told
them that as he proceeded he would find the name of
one of the men originally engaged in depositing the
treasure, engraved on a plate. The plate with the
name—JAMES LONG—had now been found, at least
such was his belief, though the man who discovered it
did not like to show it, but rather preferred to keep
them in the lively exercise of faith. The treasure
buried was none other than the long-sought treasure
of the Pirate Kidd. It lay under a black marble
slab, thirty feet square, and beautifully polished, resting on corner-stones, with a ring-bolt in the centre.
They were sure to have it in three days.

Having thus delivered himself, and finding that I
was not disposed to bid high for his claim, he cooled

off, and, instead of digging in the excavation with his friends, very prudently went away into a corner of his clearing and began to hoe potatoes. But the others showed a more genuine faith, and continued to ply their spades, at the same time expressing their happy expectation. For himself, Graybeard did not follow the example of the man who had just left me for his hoe. *He* made no secret of it with *any* one. He expected *gold*. He was at work for a good paymaster, who would pay when the work was done. I fervently hoped that it was so; but then, would his work ever be *done?* The notion was scorned. There could be no mistake. The treasure was already within their grasp. He had talked with Kidd, and knew all about it; and so he plied his spade with fresh zeal.

This was the end of the controversy, and we prepared to leave. Whereupon one of the diggers came out of the hole and inquired for "the axe," and began to circle about a small tree under which Amarinta sat, all the while in his gyrations approaching nearer and nearer. Accordingly Amarinta became alarmed, and rushed out of the charmed circle. Of this the man took no notice; but finding his axe, instead of proceeding to slaughter, he quietly regained his hole in the ground, where we heard him beating the dents out of a shovel, preparatory to a fresh raid upon the inexhaustible treasures of Robert Kidd.

Thus we came off whole, notwithstanding the proprietor told Aureole that he had twenty loaded muskets standing just inside his door, an announcement that made him feel nervous. As we turned and left the diggers in the wild glen, Mr. Oldstyle tried to calculate how much gold they might have actually found if they had devoted the weeks spent upon this huge excavation to honest tillage; while, when we reached the boat, Aureole found his voice, and struck up,

"My name was Captain Kidd, as I sailed, as I sailed."

The next place on the west side is the Crows' Nest, the north spur of Dog Mountain, which descends abruptly into bold water, covered with scraggy woods from the summit down to the shore. Opposite, and now near at hand, on the east side, is Mount Mansell, which, with the Crows' Nest, forms the Narrows. The view is singularly fine, and after sailing through, the prospect widens, the sound being about three miles from shore to shore. On the east side is seen the little inlet called, like a larger bay on the west side of the island, Seal Cove. Here they formerly caught seal in abundance, but now a fish-house signifies that the chief product is herring or menhaden. On the west shore, a little way from the Crows' Nest, is a granite slide called Denning's Walk. It covers a large area, and dips to the water at a sharp angle, being beautifully embossed with moss and lichen, while here and there a small spruce struggles for life in some narrow fissure of the rock. A long while ago, on a dark winter night, a vessel was driven upon the shelving rock and went to pieces, one of the crew saving himself from freezing to death by walking on the slide until daylight.

As we sail upward the land around us sinks nearly to the level of the water, giving glimpses of the more distant mountains, while the spire of Somesville, erelong, peeps out from among the trees. From the Crows' Nest to this place is about three miles. We enter the little harbor near the head of the sound by passing through a narrow passage between an island and the shore and land near a shipyard that has a saw-mill attached. Everywhere from the upper part of the sound we have beautiful views, Mount Mansell sinking down into comparative obscurity, while Sargent's Mountain and Green Mountain loom up finely beyond the intervening woods.

Towards the east a branch of the sound extends a little higher up, and there vessels resort to load with lumber; while at Somesville it receives the fresh water that flows down from the outlets of Long Lake, on its way turning the ancient mill-wheels, which, like river-gods at enforced service, laboriously grind and saw.

Somes' Sound enables us to sail through the heart of the best scenery on the island, to which it gives a general introduction, thus preparing us to take up other portions of this wonderful place in detail. Wherever the boatman voyages, the eye is delighted by new and ever-changing views, pleasant valleys—the home of the deer—inviting us ashore for a ramble, while the mountains pencil their features around us on the waves.

With a good breeze, a sail of a couple of hours will take visitors back to South-west Harbor, though whoever has the time will find it profitable to remain at Somesville for several days.

AMONG THE MOUNTAINS.

CHAPTER VI.

Western Mountain — Beech Mountain — Storm Cliff — Dog Mountain — Climbing — A Story — Flying Mountain — The French — Sargent's Mountain.

OUNTAINS form one of the grandest features of this island; and Somes' Sound, by dividing them into two general groups, affords a convenient classification.

All the mountains on the west side are best reached from South-west Harbor, while those on the east, with the exception of Mount Mansell and Sargent's Mountain, should generally be ascended from Bar Harbor. On the west side are Western, Beech, Dog, and Flying Mountains, of which we are first to speak. These mountains may be distinguished from the others by a more verdant aspect, and a heavier growth of wood. The name of Western Mountain indicates its position on the west shore of the island, overlooking Penobscot Bay. Seen from the water, it has a tolerably sharp peak, which, as we sail around the island, assumes somewhat the form of a sugar-loaf, apparently with a tendency to topple over towards the east. Yet this cone is very firmly fixed in its place, and will never cause alarm.

From South-west Harbor the mountain is very easily reached, as a carriage-road extends for a large portion of the way, changing to a wood-road on its side, which eventually fades out. This mountain has no great reputation, yet it is in every respect a beautiful height, affording a fine view of Penobscot Bay. Seal Cove Pond, a large and handsome sheet of water, lies along its eastern side, bathing its feet and reflecting its image at times as in a glass. From the pond, the sides of the mountain sweep upward like the sides of an amphitheatre, the wood-crowned ledges rising tier on tier.

Beech Mountain is far more popular than Western Mountain, from which it is separated by Long Lake. The same road that leads to the latter will conduct us to the former, if we are careful to turn in season to the right. The mountain road passes completely over between the two highest peaks, and descends northward to the village of Somesville. On the summit, and along the south side, it is extremely rough, and not adapted to public travel, yet with a strong wagon it is passable. This route is the one that would naturally be selected, and yet to ascend from Somesville is more pleasing. It involves eight or nine miles of additional travel, but whoever has the time to spare will not regret the labor. The road to Somesville is nearly seven miles long, and thence, turning to the left, it is two and a half miles to the first peak, called the Nipple. The ascent is very gradual, and the hill is round as a whale's back. It is covered with fields, farms, and grass-lands. and on the latter were whole seas of buttercups and daisies, waving in rare beauty before the morning sun. We came this way ourselves, and as we ascended it was delightful to study each new expanding scene. Reaching the base of the first peak, we left our carriage and walked to the top, where the prospect proved quite enchanting. Northward, the mountain descended gently to Somesville; beyond were the Narrows, where the island keeps tryst with the main, which here is fenced in by some low but fine hills; eastward lay Denning's Lake, the peaks of Dog Mountain, the Gold-Diggers' Glen, Somes' Sound bordered by green woods and buttressed in the centre by Mansell, and beyond were the heights of Goldsborough, smiling upon the encircling bay: westward we marked the graceful summit of Blue Hill, the distant reaches of Penobscot Bay gemmed with fair isles and crowned by the Camden Heights; while directly before us were the slopes of Western Mountain, rising gracefully from the shadowy waters of Long Lake, which slumbered in peace at our feet.

Descending, we regained the road, and went on to still higher ground. turning to the left among the fields, and working our way on foot towards the eastern summit, near which we looked down one of those tremendous cliffs abounding in this island, and viewed the waters of Denning's Lake. Storm Cliff is of great height, and, like those of Dog Mountain, it drops perpendicularly to the water, the face being totally inaccessible. It appears to the finest advantage, however, from the opposite side of the lake, which is skirted by the Somesville road, and the passer may thus get a glimpse of it through the trees. But it is best to go down to the edge of the lake, where the cliff rises directly in front in all its majesty. When lashed by the storms, which rave around these hills with the fury of fallen angels, the view is sublime. How do the misty battalions charge upon the living rock, and then break and fly! There is certainly a soul in them; and even now the memory of a stormy day on that shore allures me down from sunny slopes and shady ridges to view once more their great conflicts.

But there is a third peak of Beech Mountain to climb, and when we leave the rough road and scale this granite cone, it becomes no trifling work. Amarinta could not do it, and so was left for a little while to the companionship of a couple of kind, motherly-looking cows, and I scrambled up to the top. From the summit of a rock all that was seen from the first peak now appeared in fresh beauty, with the additional prospect of the opening towards the south, which revealed South-west Harbor, the mouth of Somes' Sound, Bass Harbor, the eastern islands, and the boundless sea.

It would have been a pleasure to delay here for hours, but it was necessary to descend. Nor did I get back any too soon, for while I was gone an unruly steer joined the peaceful party left below, lashing his tail at the air so furiously, that Amarinta had taken possession of the reins, and was about to drive off and leave me to tramp home on foot. We returned to South-west Harbor, by the way of the rough mountain road, greatly delighted with the trip.

Dog Mountain is the local name of the eminence rising on the border of the sound. From one position towards the south it appears to be an immense mass of granite, nearly flat on the top, and with no comeliness to recommend it. On the Somesville road, near Denning's Lake, we get some idea of its altitude, and catch a glimpse of numerous steep, bare ledges; but it will not be appreciated until thoroughly climbed. The reader has already been introduced to one of its cliffs, and the Gold-Diggers' Glen, yet there is much remaining that will repay study.

The height of this, as well as of the other mountains, except Green Mountain and Newport, is not known, and we are only left to conjecture. Dog Mountain falls below Beech Mountain in altitude, yet, rising as it does directly from the water, not an inch is lost in the general effect by the interference of other objects. This, indeed, is an advantage possessed by all these sea-girt mountains, which, while lower than the Catskills, always equal and often exceed them in effect.

The ascent of Dog Mountain is easier than that of any of the higher peaks. Three quarters of an hour from South-west Harbor, taking the right-hand road to Fernald's Point, will bring a good walker to the place where he begins the ascent, which is near the valley, terminating in the cove. The route lies through sheep-walks and over bare ledges, and is occasionally obstructed by small spruces or pines. Keeping well to the right, the escarpment of the cliffs is reached, and the way is plain to the highest peaks.

Gaining the first elevation, we find that it terminates in a lofty precipice called Eagle Cliff, turning away from the sound and facing the beautiful valley formed by Flying Mountain, which now appears scarcely higher than a molehill. I climbed it alone on the Fourth of July. The sun was intensely hot, sufficiently so, indeed, to nearly boil one's brains How grateful was the cool breeze along this magnificent height, and how lovely the view both on the sound and at sea!

The last half a mile was a scramble over great disjointed rocks upheaved in the Titanic past, and here and there covered with dense thickets. At last I reached the apex, marked by a rude cairn, to which every right-minded tourist is expected to contribute a stone. On looking about, it is found that this mountain is the most barren of the western group, and that, instead of being flat-topped, it has a well-defined peak rising far above the first landing-place, which had the appearance of being the summit. The view towards the west is shut in, more or less, by Beach Mountain. Denning's Lake, which lies so near at the west, is invisible. The finest views are had up. and down the sound. Here we are able to look into the neighboring valleys and ravines and inspect the physical peculiarities of this highland region, which is everywhere deeply scarred by the old geological agents. The development of the trap-rock is very marked. Intrusions, varying in width from three to thirty feet, may be traced along the axis of elevation. In one place I noticed that the face of the trap had been laid bare by a fault in the granite, exposing an immense wall forty or fifty feet high. These veins may undoubtedly be traced for miles, their extent indicating the vast destructive powers which nature has in store, powers that, if unchained, would soon cause all the elements to hiss and bubble in the fervent heat.

What studies in rock are here unfolded to the painter, as well as to the geologist! How gloriously crag is piled on crag, now laid firmly together with masonic skill, and now gaping with seams and rents, instantly threatening to fall!

With reluctance I rose from my hard couch under the shadow of the cairn, and, after casting a farewell glance into the Gold-Diggers' Glen, so replete with romantic beauty, I began my tramp downward. Reaching the brow of the precipice overlooking the cove, I paused again, enchanted by the beauty of the scene. It was now high noon, the breeze had died away, and a dead calm prevailed. The sound lay before me smooth as a sea of glass; nearer was the green cove, where the brick-red cows sought the shade of the rocks: while Flying Mountain rose up beyond like some fair green altar prepared for sacrifice. All sounds around me were hushed in this hour of noontide calm, and only the report of an occasional Liberty gun came booming across the waters of Penobscot Bay. I sat here long to gaze upon this scene of enchantment, and at the same time called to mind an incident about the cliff which was told me one day by a farmer as we walked in the cove below, considering the all-absorbing question of buried gold.

Looking up at these granite walls, I asked if it was possible to scale them. He replied that it was not, though he had been able to make his way up at the side. One of his sheep, it appears, had slipped part way down the cliff, and alighted upon a projecting ledge. The poor creature was unable to extricate herself from this perilous position, not having the power to get either up or down. Here upon this narrow pasture, where a sudden blast might whirl her off, and make mutton of her on the cruel rocks hundreds of feet below, she managed to browse for nearly a fortnight, subsisting upon moss and accidental moisture, while her piteous cries daily fell fainter and fainter in the farmer's ear. At last a man, moved with pity, volunteered on Sunday afternoon to attempt a rescue. Armed with a long pole, he tried to make his way down to the ledge, and when last seen he was lying upon his face, searching out a passage. A minute afterwards those anxiously watching him suddenly found that he had disappeared. The discovery filled them with consternation. Looking above they could not see him retreating, and the conclusion was, that he had fallen unobserved, and was dashed in pieces. The alarm was raised, the neighbors assembled, and after a diligent but fruitless search, they concluded to give it up. But before returning, they raised a united shout, calling the man by name, if, haply, he might still be alive. And the echo had hardly died away when the man came out through the bushes of the cove and stood unharmed before them. Here was a miracle? Not quite; for, instead of tumbling down the cliff, he became frightened and crawled back through a crevice in the rock, afterwards descending the opposite side of the mountain to visit a neighbor, from whose house he was now returning home. The people felt greatly relieved, though somewhat foolish; but the faint cry of the poor sheep still floated down from her narrow prison. It was accordingly resolved to make a fresh attempt, and a rope having been provided, a sailor was let down to the ledge. After some effort, he brought up the famished creature in his arms. As for the brave fellow himself, he was drowned but a little while ago. On a cold winter night his vessel was running for Squam Light in a thick snow-storm, when she struck the beach, bilged, and burned up.

So much for the story; and now here were the cliffs before me, gray, steep, and perilous as ever. And could I get down? *Hoc labor est.* I certainly thought the difficulty had been overrated and began to beat about in every possible place to find some way to descend. But after cautiously trying a hundred and fifty feet the difficulty grew more and more apparent, and the way was at last barred by one of those perpendicular walls of granite that yield to no argument or persuasion. Discretion was here the better part of valor, and accordingly I climbed back to the summit again, where I caught the faint halloo of a boating-party on the strand. They saw me up among the crags, reduced in the distance to a speck, and sent up their salutations. They acknowledged my own with a waving of hats; but Echo took it up and sent it back with perfect distinctness from the far-off sides of Mount Mansell. Just then a light breeze swept down through the cove, kissed the white sails of the little yacht, and bore her away.

Flying Mountain is a pigmy among the hills, yet here the lover of the beautiful would build his chateau. It was observed, as a matter of course, in our trip up the sound, but it now requires more particular consideration. Its situation is unequalled. It seems as if placed here to afford the best possible out-look upon the lovliest scenery of the sound. The approach is quite romantic. Soon after leaving the turn of the road at the head of South-west Harbor, the mountain lifts itself up to great advantage beyond the fields, yet when we reach a given point near the cove it affords a pleasing surprise, breaking into view through the trees, with a part of Dog Mountain appearing on the left.

It is moreover a place that all can visit. Mr. Oldstyle was delighted because it was historic ground; yet he confessed that its easy slopes suited his legs. He would none of your tramps and forced marches through tangled woods and dells. That would do for poachers and boys. He often shook his head at our folly. But now he felt that he had an object before him. This was the beautiful hill of Father Biard, of Masse, and of Brother Gilbert du Thet. So, planting his gold-mounted stick in the compact soil, he nimbly trod the beaten path of the woolly sheep and ascended to the summit, where he seated himself upon a rock, and, slightly accommodating a quotation from Shakspeare, delivered himself as follows:

> "This *Mountain* hath a pleasant seat; the air
> Nimbly and sweetly recommends itself
> Unto our gentle senses."

Thereupon he laid aside his broad-brimmed hat, and allowed the soft summer breeze to wander at will among his locks. We left him to view at leisure the green fields below, where the French built their little fort, set up their tents, raised the Cross, sang the *Mass*, and chanted *Vexilla regis prodeunt;* to look down upon the calm waters of the sound, where Argall's ship came on "swift as an arrow," pouring in her broadside against the French; to see du Thet springing to the guns with the spirit of a hero, but quickly falling to welter in his own blood; to see the unequal fight, the speedy surrender, the pillage of the tents, the solemn funeral of the slain, and, finally, the departure of Argall, leaving the devastated camp wreathed in smoke. These things have now all passed away, yet to our antiquarian friend they are vivid realities. Gilbert du Thet's ashes rest somewhere beneath yonder greensward, the spring from which he drank still flows out from under the loins of this hill, the mountains upon which he gazed remain, the same ocean breaks upon the shore, and the same stars and sky look down from above. A single effort of the imagination re-creates the scene. So let us give Mr. Oldstyle a few minutes to himself, and we will scramble along the ridge of the mountain, which now assumes a wilder aspect, being broken up and seamed with trap, and sentinelled here and there with the half-burnt trunks of pine.

At the termination of the ridge the mountain descends abruptly to the sound, leaving no beach. It is therefore impracticable to pass around on the water side, except with a boat. The view of the neighboring mountains from this point is most lovely. It seems as if one could almost throw a stone up among the crags of Eagle Cliff opposite, while Thunder Cliff bears on its front the characteristics of a palisade. Sweeping away towards the middle of the sound is the north spur of Dog Mountain, while Mount Mansell, in a friendly mood, seems to advance from the east. Here we have a fresh view of the jutting cliffs of the Gold-Digger's Glen, and mark the seamed sides of the distant heights, which are written all over with records of the Ancient of Days. Towards sunset the view will perhaps appear to the best advantage, as at that time the lengthening shadows bring out more clearly the structure of the neighboring cliffs, while the red granite bosses of Sargent and Green Mountain assume a softer glow. From this place we can look away in any direction landward, and peep into pictured alcoves and down shining vistas, or, turning from the mountains, gaze across the sunlit islands upon the purple sea. All is sweetness, beauty and repose.

I selected Somesville as the point of departure for Sargent's Mountain on the east side of the sound. The ascent can be accomplished by crossing the sound from South-west Harbor, yet few persons, when at Somesville, will be able to resist the temptation to make a trip to this inviting height, which lifts itself up in the distance before the door of the little home-like hotel. The foot of the mountain may be reached either by boat or carriage. In the latter case it will be necessary to take the road to North-east Harbor. The route by water is pleasanter, as it affords charming glimpses down the sound. A brisk row of three-fourths of an hour brings us to a place called Seal Cove, like one of the inlets on the west shore of the island, where seals were formerly taken in abundance. Here we left the boat, struck across the fields, and found a wood road running along the base of the mountain. My guide evidently knew as little about the route as I did, yet I thought it well to have him along. Some men who were hoeing potatoes replied to my inquiries in a way that showed a slight degree of contempt for city folk. They "guessed," too, that I meant to stay on the mountain all night, thereby intending to reflect on the judgment exhibited in commencing the ascent in the middle of the afternoon. Unable to learn anything from these churls, who had lived here all their lives, we pursued the wood road until it became reduced to a sort of squirrel-track, and then moved straight up the pathless side of the mountain. Thickets, dense foliage, and fallen trees everywhere obstructed the way, and a hard struggle was often required in order to open a passage. Occasionally the steep ledges intervened, from which glimpses were had of the expanding prospect, while it often appeared as if the summit lay within a few rods. Yet for a long, toilsome hour and a half, ledge rose on ledge. Finally the apex was reached and the reward gained. Every way the prospect exceeded my anticipations. From a distance the summit of the mountain appeared round and smooth, but when actually climbed it was found to be the most broken and rugged eminence on the island, and at the same time the most barren and desolate. The top occupies a large area full of rifts that, lower down, assume the character of chasms and ravines, among which everything except the sky is frequently lost to view. Mount Mansell, which lies between Sargent's Mountain and the sound, is scarcely seen from the northern part of the summit, the view being obstructed by a spur of Sargent that is separated from the main peak by a wild ravine with nearly perpendicular walls. Eastward, however, there is a fine view of Green Mountain brought out in bold relief by the declining sun.

Following the ridge of Sargent's Mountain southward about half a mile, a view of Eagle Lake is had, lying far down among the hills in the shade, and sparkling, at the evening hour, like a black diamond. A little farther south, in a cup-like depression of the ridge, is the Lake of the Clouds, a small body of water about an acre in extent, and which, according to fable has no bottom. Yet a line let down from a raft once gave a depth of sixteen feet. It is supplied chiefly by the winter snows. This lake lies in what resembles an ancient crater, though the rock is of granite and no signs of volcanic action are visible. Indeed, every thing indicates the action of ice and frost. Agassiz, when here, noted the resemblance of this mountain to the Swiss hills that have been shaped by glacial action. The summit is everywhere worn and rounded by vast icefields five or six thousand feet thick, which the great savan tells us crushed their way down from the high regions of Katahdin to the sea. No less stupendous a force could have accomplished such results.

From this part of the mountain the view is open towards the south, giving a view of Hadlock and Jordan's Ponds, North-east Harbor, and the neighboring regions, with the broad Atlantic beyond.

As I left the margin of the Lake of the Clouds, the sun threw his slanting beams against the rose-colored granite wall that shuts it in on the south, when the rocks began to mirror themselves in the water, flinging down their warm tints upon the rushes and lily-pads which were growing green among the delicately penciled images of the dwarfed spruce and pine.

The descent was accomplished by a different and still more difficult route. A tolerably easy way could have been found along by Jordan's Pond, yet my destination was Somesville ; and, therefore, after scrambling downward a short distance, in a southerly direction, we took the range of prominent points on Mount Mansell and prepared to move westward down across the deep valley to the North-east Harbor road. But here the wild beauty of the scene delayed me for a little while, notwithstanding the night was coming on, and a long tramp was still to be accomplished. There, a thousand feet below, lay a long verdure-clad valley, sweeping down from the rifted summit and sides of Sargent's Mountain, into which, through rocky defiles, the setting sun threw long lances of light that only served to render the fast-gathering shade more impressive. But what proved equally beautiful was the music of the birds, which from the day I first stepped ashore at Mount Desert never ceased to prove a source of delight. And now the whole valley rang with song, and, as a dead calm prevailed, every note was caught up and echoed among the mountains, the effect being as singular as it was beautiful.

But I was soon admonished by my guide of the necessity of pushing on, and therefore I reluctantly sought the edge of the declivity and slid down from rock to rock among the trees, until I reached an open place near the centre of the valley, where I could look up at the crag which I had just left. Then, pushing into the dense woods, we beat our way through the under-brush, amidst the fast-gathering gloom, until, long after sunset, we joyfully emerged upon the road which passes under the perpendicular cliffs in the east side of Mount Mansell. The walk here in this notch is always fine, but at twilight it is unusually interesting.

A rapid walk of two miles northward brought us to the cove in Somes' Sound, where we had left the boat.

It was soon launched, and speeding on its way, impelled by two flashing oars. On this occasion I had an opportunity of witnessing the effect of a summer twilight on this beautiful sheet of water; for the sky, barred with crimson and purple, flooded the surface with its own deep hues, while Dog Mountain and Mount Mansell flung themselves darkly down at full length on the calm, pulseless tide. And out of their shadows loomed numerous spectral sails, while a light in the window of a distant cottage threw down a faint flame that vainly tried to dance upon the waves rising in our homeward track.

At half-past nine o'clock our boat grounded at the head of the sound, and soon after the kind hostess of the Mount Desert House welcomed me to a steaming supper.

AMONG THE MOUNTAINS.

CHAPTER VII.

BAR HARBOR — THE ASCENT OF GREEN — THE PROSPECT — NIGHT — A THUNDER STORM — THE DESCENT — NEWPORT — HOMER — ROUND PEAK — ECHO NOTCH — DRY MOUNTAIN — UP GREEN — BACK AGAIN.

OTWITHSTANDING the beauty of the western group, the mountains east of Somes' Sound present still greater interest and variety. Consequently they are better known, and more thoroughly studied.

With the exception of Mansell and Sargent, they are all to be reached from the east side of the sound. Bar Harbor is the proper point of departure, and by making the ascent of Newport and Green Mountain, we can gain an acquaintance with the rest.

Of all these sea-girt mountains, Newport, after Green Mountain, is deservedly the most popular. Some persons even place Newport in the advance of Green, declaring that it has peculiar attractions for which nothing can compensate. Yet, while conceding the advantages of Newport, Green Mountain elevates itself above all the rest, both in pictorial interest and in commanding height.

In crossing the island to Bar Harbor, our friend Oldstyle, and others averse to climbing, were left behind, while new friends and acquaintances entered the circle. Here the mountain tramp is never a solitary excursion. At a signal, troops of pedestrians issue forth to explore the neighboring regions, and two or three in nearly every circle were always ready to climb the highest peak and the most difficult pass

But happily Green Mountain presents few obstacles in the way of visitors. For a number of years the officers of the Coast Survey had an Observatory on its summit, and when work was suspended a tolerable road was left, which has since been improved to such an extent that carriages can, if necessary, ascend to the top; though it is the custom for most persons to perform the last two miles on foot. The whole distance, four miles from the village, is a pleasant excursion for a pedestrian in full strength.

As we ascend, Eagle Lake comes in view on the right, lying along the flank of the mountain in a trough-like depression, while beyond the ranges rise in regular order. The view towards Newport and the sea is shut in by the woody ridge of Green Mountain, along the back-bone of which the road runs, though at several points about half way up may be had charming glimpses of Goldsborough Mountains and Frenchman's Bay. Finally, on reaching the top, a glowing prospect greets the eye, land and sea mingling in the most captivating forms. In a clear day the view is very extensive. Katahdin shows a clearly defined peak many miles distant, while Mount Washington at times will even vouchsafe to unveil its head.

On the ocean, Mount Desert Rock may be distinguished with the aid of a glass about fifteen miles distant, while a maze of beautiful islands rise up around the shores. The scene is one of great beauty. Whittier gives a sketch in his poem of *Mogg Megone*, placing his French hermit priest on one of these peaks, where, while gazing on the scene below, he

> "May half forget the dreams of home,
> That nightly with his slumbers come,—
> The tranquil skies of sunny France,
> The peasant's harvest song and dance,
> The vines around the hill-side wreathing,
> The soft airs 'midst their clusters breathing,
> The wing which dipped, the star that shone
> Within thy bosom, blue Garonne.
>   *   *   *   *   *   *
> For here before him is unrolled,
> Bathed deep in morning's flood of gold,
> A vision gorgeous as the dream
> Of the beatitudes may seem;
>   When as his Church's legends say,
> Borne upward in extatic bliss,
>   The rapt enthusiast soars away
> In a brighter world than this:
> A mortal's glimpse beyond the pale—
> A moment's lifting of the veil."

The top of Green Mountain is grooved out by two little vallies which run nearly north-west and southeast. The western valley, which descends towards the sea, is filled with small trees and shrubs. Crossing near its head and descending in a westerly direction, we reach the brow, where may be had a fine view of the wild region lying between Green Mountain and Sargent. Pemetic is seen close at hand, lifting up its sharp barren ridge; the Bubble Mountains next appear, rejoicing modestly in their green crowns of lesser height; beyond is the dark but splendid range of Sargent, shutting in the sky; while Eagle Lake stretches northward at our feet. Only the more persistent climber penetrates into these recesses of Mount Desert, where he may any day come face to face with the fierce-looking but inoffensive wild-cat, or the harmless deer. One never tires of looking down upon the dark, tangled woods, the jagged peaks, and dusky glens, where the light and shade hold perpetual play, bringing out the strongest and most beautiful effects.

Other very fine views may be had, to see which we must scramble around the entire summit. But only one of these can be mentioned here, though in some respects it is the grandest to be had on the whole island. It is seen from the north-east brow, where the visitor looks down into the Otter Creek Valley, lying between Green Mountain and its spur known as Dry Mountain. The prospect is marked both by variety and magnitude. Immediately before us is the valley, a thousand feet deep, clothed in dark green forests, well-watered in the centre by a cool, invisible brook, and terminating in the blue fiord of Otter

Creek; beyond is the ridge of Dry Mountain and the peak of Newport, rising in bold relief against the sea; while to the left, far down upon the shore, is the village of Bar Harbor, fronting the isles and waters of Frenchman's Bay. Language cannot fitly convey an adequate impression of the beauty of this scene, which when once viewed will linger forever in the memory.

It was a beautiful July morning when we made our first excursion to the summit, in company with a merry party. Occasionally we saw the glacial marks on the rocks, that Agassiz views as records of the Ice-period in Maine; but we were chiefly interested in the prospect, which unfolded some fresh charm at every step. On reaching the summit we were denied a view of the more distant objects, such as Katahdin and Mount Washington, which are seen only in remarkable clear weather, but objects far out at sea were distinctly visible. We enjoyed a beautiful sunset, yet as night came on the fog rolled in from the sea, shutting out the view of the numerous beacon lights that twinkle on the coast. Only the light on Bear Island appeared at intervals.

The world below being wrapped in darkness, we were obliged to confine ourselves to the little house erected here for the entertainment of visitors. It is a rough-built structure, thrown together on the umbrella principle, with all the framework showing on the inside, being braced up without by light timbers of spruce planted in the rock to enable it to withstand the heavy gales. The little parlor in the centre is flanked by the dining-room, and a couple of dormitories, while overhead, in a loft, a double tier of berths is arranged, steamboat fashion, for the further accommodation of the disciples of Morpheus. During those cold, stormy nights which occur on the mountain even in the middle of July, the well-filled stove is no unwelcome companion, but tends to promote jollity in the circle of wayfarers usually gathered around it. Here, when supper is over, the adventures of the day are recited, the song is sung, and the story told, while the walls at times will crack with peals of laughter.

At an early hour the weary pedestrian usually retires, with a firm resolution to be up betimes and receive the first greetings of Old Sol as he rises from his ocean bed. Our company followed the custom of the place, though not before some young sons of Yale had executed a grand bear dance on the rough board floor in the loft which had been assigned to their use. Mine host looked slightly aghast when he heard the timbers groaning about his ears, but on being assured that the party was no less safe than noisy and "all right," he took a candle and sought his downy couch, simply enjoining us to put out the lights when we got ready.

The tired Collegians, however, had hardly ended their performance on the light fantastic toe, when a fearful thunder-storm arose, which set the sky all ablaze and made the mountains reel. When morning came no glorious sunrise greeted our eye, but the heavens were still pealing, while the lightning seemed fairly to rain down upon every part of the country below. It was one of those storms such as the inhabitant of Mount Desert experiences but once in a lifetime, being tropical both in its characteristics and disastrous effects.

When breakfast was over the storm abated, and we went forth to view as much of the prospect as could be discerned through the mist. The rain had fallen in floods, and the cascades were tearing over the rocks and shooting down the steep ledges, while the fog veiling Otter Creek Valley only occasionally opened and gave a glimpse of the half-drowned woods below.

Soon the most of the party grew weary of watching the fog, and all but two departed for Bar Harbor. By four o'clock in the afternoon my own patience was exhausted. and in the midst of a driving gale and blinding fog, Amarinta and I left the house, started down the deluged road. and pushed on without pausing, until at the end of an hour and a half we entered the hotel at Bar Harbor. Thus, for the time, ended our dreams of Green Mountain.

Several days after, while the ledges in the mountain were still glistening with mimic cascades, we ascended beautiful Newport, which from every point of view appears a perfect picture. In form, it is the most symmetrical of the mountains, while it has just verdure enough to set off its splendid cliffs to great advantage.

Just below the junction of the Otter Creek and Schooner-Head Roads, a cart-track leads away to the right towards the foot of Newport, terminating in a path, which turns to the left and runs up to the lowest ridge. Reaching this path, the climber makes his way upward. Soon the spur on the right, known as Round Peak, assumes a definite form, and the ocean appears on the left. Little cairns piled up at intervals now indicate the way.

An hour's climbing brought my two companions and myself to the highest peak, surmounted by a pyramid of stones. Here we took a brief rest and disposed of our lunch, which was washed down with liberal draughts of rain water found in the depressions of the rock, and, which being bitter, we called lichen broth. To sweeten such a vegetable compound would require the skill of a Moses. But even this beverage is found only after a rain, while of living springs there are none. My sentimental friend will say that these are carnalities, yet nothing adds less to the enjoyment of Newport than a hungry stomach, or a burning thirst.

One charm of Newport Mountain is found in its nearness to the ocean. Only a narrow strip of land intervenes between its base and the sea. From its summit we could look down upon the deck of a passing steamer, the Lewiston, sailing for South-west Harbor. The jagged drongs of Egg Rock were goring the breakers like so many mad bulls, while Schoodic Point and the coast of Maine lay shining in the sun. Elsewhere all was filled up by the restless waves.

Inland lay Green Mountain, covering the more distant heights with its huge bulk. My friend The Scholar, recently let loose from Yale, was fond of pocket editions of the classics; and on the way up he had labored to show us the resemblance of Homer's *Poluphloisboio Thallassas* to the voice of the loud-sounding sea. But now, as we lay under the shadow of the cairn, the *Iliad* was drawn forth from a side-pocket, where it had balanced the opposite luncheon-box, to perform a new service. The Scholar thought and herein we agreed with him, that one line conveyed admirably the characteristics of Mount Desert. Homer speaks of the "very many shadowy mountains and the resounding sea"; "And now," said The Scholar "just look at Green Mountain!" We enthusiastically applauded the idea. The old Bard photographs both the isles of Greece and Mount Desert heights.[1]

But a long tramp was before us, and we did not delay to view the two lesser peaks of Newport which break the long range in its descent to the sea at Otter

(1)—Οὐ γὰρ ἐγὼ Τρώων ἕνεκ' ἤλυθον αἰχμητάων
δεῦρο μαχησόμενος· ἐπεὶ οὔτιμοι αἴτιοί εἰσιν.
οὐ γὰρ πώποτ' ἐμὰς βοῖς ἤλασαν, οὐδὲ μὲν ἵππους,

Creek; nor to view "Loch Anna," a little body of water named by Church, who saw it set like a diamond in the lower spur. With regret we bade adieu to this romantic height, where the earth and sky seem so much in love with one another, and began the toilsome descent westward down over the steep cliffs and through the pathless woods. Finally we touched the lower spur of Round Peak, and then pushed vigorously on, until we struck the Otter Creek road, and found ourselves in Echo Notch, which is walled in by the steep sides of Dry Mountain. Here, overshadowed by the towering cliffs, one almost fancies himself in the White Mountain Notch. In a calm day the echo is splendid. Some verses composed for *Lippincott's Magazine* so well describe the place that they may be given here:

> " Grim mountain Sprite! that, robed in woods,
>   Dost sit among these hills, their rightful King,
>   Forgive the wight who rashly dares
>   To vex thy silence with his questioning.

οἰδέ ποτ' εν Φϑίῃ ἐριβώλακι, βωτιανείρῃ,
καρπὸν ἐδηλήσαντ'· ἐπείμάλα πολλ μεταξὺ
οὔρεά τε σκιόεντα, ϑάλλασσά τε ἠχήεσσα.
                                   ILIAD, B. I., l. 152.

Well dost thou know that 't was no feud of mine,
With Troy's brave sons that brought me here in arms;
They never did me wrong; they never drove
My cattle or my horses; never sought
In Phthia's fertile, life-sustaining fields,
To waste the crops; for wide between us lay
The shadowy mountains and the roaring sea.
                        DERBY'S TRANSLATION.

> Adown thy steep and rugged flanks
> The black fir glooms and the pale aspens quiver,
> And o'er thy glistening, wind-swept cliffs,
> The mossy, perfumed streamlets leap forever.
>
> We call to thee; our feeble cry
> Dies 'gainst the rocky faces of thy throne;
> And from the shaggy bosom comes
> Thine answer, deep-voiced as an organ tone.
>
> In that broad breast no human heart
> To human pulses answereth again:
> The wandering wretch, in wood-paths lost,
> To thy stern face for pity looks in vain.
>
> Within that Sphinx-like face we fain
> Would read the riddle of life's fleeting story—
> Thy calm eternal would we grasp,
> And gild our gloom with thy far-shining glory.
>
> But thou! Thou gazest on the sea,
> With fir-crowned, stony brow that changes never:
> We leave thee, in dumb mystery,
> Dread Sprite! to heave that hoary bulk forever."

Our destination was the top of Green Mountain, and another scramble was inevitable. Therefore, without much delay, we struck through the pretty strip of wood skirting the foot of the eminence, found a narrow wooded ravine, and, keeping where we could take advantage of the trees, worked our way up. From the foot of the mountain we saw little more than what appeared an almost perpendicular granite wall, but we were gratified to find this convenient groove, though it was filled up with immense masses of fallen rocks, over which we were forced to climb. After an hour's labor we were finally able to overlook the peak of Newport and view the sea. In a quarter

of an hour more we were on the top of this spur,
called Dry Mountain, picking blueberries and seeking
for the best way across the ravine which separated us
from Green. We finally decided to take the most
shallow part of the ravine and push straight across.
At this place the mountain appears to have been split
in two, leaving the steep walls facing each other on
either hand. To get down the east side is nearly as
difficult as to get up the west, while at every step we
were in danger of dislodging huge masses of rock that
needed scarcely more than a finger's touch to send
them thundering below. Where the operation was
safe we found it capital sport, but prudence taught us
on these occasions to keep close together, lest some
flying boulder should sweep one of us into the black
ravine. At the bottom is a dense forest of spruce and
fir; and among the loose rocks, covered in some places
to the depth of nearly a foot with soft, green, spongy
moss, was a small, ice-cold stream, tinkling musically
on its way to Otter Creek. In this shady chasm,

> "An hydeous hole al vaste, withouten shape,
> Of endless depth, orewhelmde with ragged stone,"

the atmosphere was as frigid as the water, and, with
chattering teeth, we again sought the soft summer air.
But now we found the hardest climb of all. The
Scholar, quite forgetting Homer and the "shadowy
mountains," flung his stalwart frame against the iron
cliffs and gave us a splendid illustration of muscular

Christianity, while our legal friend, erst a crack oarsman of Yale, and tough as steel, made an equally powerful demonstration; but the slippery rocks were at times perfectly inexorable, and we were frequently forced to climb the trees and swing ourselves up. Finally, we surmounted this tremendous barrier, and, gasping for breath, sat down to rest.

But the sunset view from the summit was still before us, and we soon hastened up along the ledges towards the Green Mountain House, delaying however, at the right point for a parting glance at Otter Creek Valley, which was fast filling up with the sombre shade.

As we neared the house, mine Host appeared from behind the wood-pile with an armful of sticks. We bade him hail, and bespoke a fire, which was soon crackling in the stove, adding much to our comfort. Supper likewise tended to put us in a mood to enjoy the evening pyrotechnics of Old Sol, and while he was preparing to draw the bright curtains of the clouds around him and plunge out of sight, we took our sticks and wearily began the trudge down the rough mountain road. This journey is one that always repays the investment of muscle, though it is never more enjoyable than at the evening hour. How beautifully does the prospect unfold itself! Eagle Lake shimmering in the golden light, the birds-eye view of Somes' Sound and Blue Hill, the dismantled, half-spectral pines, Sargent's gray and dusky sides, numberless green valleys and lesser hill-tops, and the islanded and purpling waters of Frenchman's Bay— all these combine to form a most enchanting picture which assumes new combinations and produces exquisite effects at every turn in the winding road. Along the lower slopes, however, the daylight disappeared, and through the opening in the woods we saw the stars being slowly lighted up; while the nighthawks circled around our heads, uttering what at this hour always seems such a mournful cry. Bringing off as I did a heavy sprain as a souvenir of the tramp, I gave way slightly to the influences of the hour and walked on in silence at a little distance behind my friends, whom I heard discussing all sorts of subjects, beginning with "Culprit Fay," and ending with the respective merits of Theology and Law. The disciple of Blackstone stoutly averred that the Law made men remarkably exact, while Theology tended to looseness, there being no opposition counsel in court to pick him in pieces. Of course his view was duly refuted; though for my own part I thought that both were about half right. I mention this simply to show the turn which thought often takes here, the morning fancy often ending in questions of fact. Two hours after sunset we reached home.

Next to Green Mountain, on the west, is Pemetic, so called for the purpose of perpetuating the Indian name of Mount Desert. It extends south-eastwardly from the end of Eagle Lake, and gradually sinks down towards the sea, presenting a sharp granite ridge, which, when viewed from the north, faintly cleaves the sky. It may be reached from Bar Harbor by the way of the Otter Creek road, yet the journey is too long. The short route is to ascend Eagle Lake and climb its steep side. Landing on one of the two white sand beaches at the head of the lake, we struck into the woods, keeping just within the border of the old forest, as the recent growth is well nigh impassable, on account of the dense thickets.

Glancing at the mountain, we concluded that half an hour would be sufficient to take us to the top. Yet we were greatly disappointed, erring both in regard to the height to be climbed and the difficulties to be encountered. The fallen timber disputed our progress at nearly every step, while for about three quarters of an hour the summit continued to recede. Still we scrambled on, and, after getting clear of the woods, made our way from ledge to ledge, until we stood upon the topmost of the series, which terminate on the east side in perpendicular walls.

Nearly an hour and a half was consumed in reaching the summit of Pemetic, which is both grand and bare. It is sufficiently high to afford a glimpse of the Green Mountain House on the east, and a full view of the recesses of Sargent and the Bubble Mountains. Northward is the lake, and more distant the region around Trenton Bridge, while southward is a superb view of the islands and the sea. The islands probably appear to better advantage from this point than any other. On Green Mountain the tourist is too far above them and the details are lost; but here the floating masses of pale green assume a definite character, and profitably employ the eye.

Still what most impressed us was the wildness of the scene. The upper portion of Pemetic is a mass of rose-colored granite descending eastward in a series of long gigantic steps; while the half-covered sides of Green Mountain combine with the positive desolation of Sargent to complete the rugged character of the view and fill it with romantic interest. Jordan's Pond also adds an important feature, lying cradled under the cliffs of Sargent, dark and threatening, and appearing altogether as if it would like to drown one. This is a splendid place in which to pass the day, or to camp at night, while to the artist or photographer it is worth a fortune.

The deer are still found in the mountains. Last summer a Harvard student found a pair of antlers on Pemetic. As is well known, they shed them every year, at least until they reach old age; which is the case with the moose, who throws off antlers weighing from twenty-five to fifty pounds as easily as a Jew puts off "old clo'." The deer swim off to the island from the main-land every fall to escape the dogs that are set to driving them out of the woods. Forty years ago, I am told, the deer were strangers to the place; and if the hunting were stopped in the neighboring regions they would soon disappear from the island. But, as it is, fresh stock comes on every autumn. The Oldtown Indians resort here every season to hunt them, in connection with the otter, fox, wild-cat, muskrat, and mink. The law allows the deer to be hunted for three months, ending with the fifteenth of December. In coming here the Indians simply followed the custom of their ancestors. The old chroniclers occasionally mention their visits, as is the case with Hubbard, who connects it with the captivity of young Cobelt, son of the minister at Ipswich, Massachusetts, who was taken prisoner by the Indians, near Portland, in 1677. He was afterwards taken by his " pateroon," or master, to Mount Desert, where he was accustomed to spend his winters, and arrange his hunting expeditions. Hubbard says: " In that desert-like condition was the poor young man forced to continue nine weeks in the service of a savage miscreant, who sometimes would tyrannize over him, because he could not understand his language, and for want thereof might occasion him to miss his game, or the like." At the end of nine weeks " on a sudden he took a resolution to send this young man down to Penobscot to Mr. [Baron] Casteen to procure more powder to kill moose and deer, which it seems is all their way of living at Mount Desert." This journey led to his ransom, which was finally effected by being exchanged for a good coat. Hubbard tells us how that on one occasion while a prisoner on the island he went out to hunt, and was so overcome by the cold that he became senseless, and that the Indians were obliged to take him on their shoulders and carry him to the nearest wigwam. Formerly, also, the beaver was plenty here, as is still attested by the remains of their dams.

Between Pemetic and Sargent lie the Bubble Mountains, or Twins. The larger of the two heights stands at the head, or north end of Jordan's Pond, and the other advances along the eastern side. They form the two principal peaks of a ridge lying on the west side of Eagle Lake. Between this ridge and Sargent's Mountain is a narrow valley rising at its northern extremity even with the lesser elevation, and furnishing an additional water-shed to Jordan's Pond. The whole region between Eagle Lake and Sargent's Mountain is covered with a dense forest of somewhat recent growth that effectually bars every approach to The Twins.

One day we made a party to climb them, and started from Bar Harbor at nine o'clock in the morning. Walking to Eagle Lake, we found the boats all out, and therefore tried to find our way through the woods, beating about among the bushes until high noon. At this time we gave up the attempt and divided, one party striking out westward to scale Sargent's Mountain and return home by Jordan's Pond and the Otter Creek road, while the other returned to the McFarland House to form some new plan. There I drove a hard bargain for a boat which was just returning down the lake, stipulating that when done with it should be left on the beach at the other end, from whence the owner should bring it home again at his convenience. At half past two o'clock we got into the boat and rowed up the lake against a heavy breeze and a short, chop sea, which severely taxed our strength. Landing at last on the farthest sand beach, we crossed the creek to the west, and struck up the steep side of the Bubble ridge, keeping well to the right, and touched the top after a lively scramble of twenty minutes. Starting from thence in a southerly direction through trees and underwood, ten minutes more brought us to the highest point, when the object of the expedition was declared accomplished. And the result amply repaid us for all the toil of the day, affording as it did some of the grandest views, besides an accurate knowledge of the geography of this part of the island. Westward, and far above us, lay Sargent's Mountain, holding up to our gaze its torn and rifted sides; to the north stretched what we may call the Valley of The Twins; on the east the forest cut off the prospect of Eagle Lake, while southward lay Jordan's Pond and the islands out at sea.

As we sat gazing upon the summit of Sargent, our friends whom we had left in the woods appeared in the form of two dark specks, moving along the ridge against the evening sky. One was a Harvard College undergraduate, who, the year before, rowed his wherry from Boston to Mount Desert. They had fought their way through the thickets to the top of Sargent, and were now taking a fifteen mile walk home. Quickly arranging a signal with our pocket handkerchiefs, we hoisted it on a pole, and gave a united shout. The signal was recognized, and the sound of our voices, aided by the wind, also succeeded in getting across the great gulf that separated us, and then crept up to Sargent's ridge. A faint halloo came back in reply, and then, after viewing one another for some time, we started homeward by opposite routes, our own covering as good as a dozen miles. Of the distance separating the two peaks we could form no estimate. The voice of the sentinel has been heard sounding the "All's well" from Old to New Gibraltar, a distance of nine miles; yet our own voices probably did not reach half as far.

On our return we paused a few minutes at the brink of the cliffs overlooking Eagle Lake to enjoy the beauty of the prospect here spread out before us, it being an exquisite mingling of lake, mountain, and forest, and then cautiously descended to the strand. We embarked, rowed to the Eastern shore, beached the boat, and then struck through the low ground which here skirts the foot of Green Mountain; afterwards going up its steep sides and reaching the top in an hour and a quarter. Arriving at the Mountain House we found a company duly assembled around the August fire, intending to stay over night. But as it was already sunset we bade mine Host good evening, started homeward by the road, and arrived at Bar Harbor in an hour and twenty minutes. I mention the time made for the benefit of those climbers in whose hands this book may fall.

It now only remains to speak of Kebo—little Kebo—sitting at the foot of Green Mountain, like some scholar at the feet of his master, and modestly rejoicing in its green prime. Many persons who have travelled far and near in Mount Desert may perhaps have never seen this hill, which is set away almost out of sight. Yet the walk to Kebo is one of the most enjoyable on the island. Indeed, after being surfeited with the grandeur of rugged rocks and tremendous precipices the tranquil beauty that surrounds Kebo is hailed as a welcome relief.

Taking the Green Mountain road as far as the cross-road at the school-house, and turning to the left, half an hour's walk from Bar Harbor brings us to the place where we gain the best view of Kebo. The view here is one of great loveliness, and some even, after seeing every other part of the island, have not hesitated to pronounce it the best of all. This, however, is because nothing in particular is generally expected, and the picture forms a pleasant surprise. There at the border of the fields rises this little hill, with its perpendicular eastern face, while beyond are Newport, Round Peak, Dry, and Green Mountains. All now appear verdure-clad to their very summits. Between Dry and Newport is Echo Notch, through which we can look, and at the same time have a view of the ravine which sweeps down from between Dry and Green Mountains. From this point we continue on past a couple of farm-houses until we reach a picturesque old mill, when, if we desire to climb Kebo, we must cross the stream, turn up the wood-road to the right, and follow on until the west side is gained, from whence the ascent is easily made. No path will be found until near the top, nor is one really needed, since there are so few obstacles in the way. Half or three quarters of an hour will bring the slowest walkers thither, where the most lovely panorama is spread out. Kebo has an elevation of not more than three or four hundred feet, but here we realize once more that there is no necessary connection between height and beauty. Here, too, in the favorable light, the whole region appeared clothed in living green. Even the dry Porcupines out in Frenchman's Bay, which at noon-day usually wear a barren aspect, now glowed with a deep emerald light, and the face of nature was everywhere wreathed in smiles. From this position the structure of Kebo also becomes apparent, and it is found to be a ridge with two well-defined peaks running parallel with Green and fading away on the side of Dry Mountain. Between Kebo and Green is a broad and beautiful valley; while east of the former elevation runs a bow-shaped ridge, bending westward, and reaching from the gateway of Echo Notch to the cross-road already mentioned. This ridge, marked on the map as The Gate of the Notch, is quite high and flat at its southern end, and when seen from Frenchman's Bay it seems to lie directly across the entrance to this splendid vale; yet in walking to Otter Creek the pedestrian will find that the Gate conveniently stands ajar.

In returning from Kebo, we tried to descend the cliffs on the east side, but were forced to give it up, the sheer, rocky walls being too much for us. We accordingly retraced our steps. In the fields we found Agricola, raking hay, and asked what amount of filthy lucre would induce him to give us the exclusive possession of his little pastoral paradise next season. This enchanted isle, with all its sweet nooks and romantic corners, could furnish nothing better for a summer home. With little Kebo, we bid the mountains adieu.

THE LAKE REGION.

CHAPTER VIII.

SEAL COVE POND — DENNING'S LAKE — STORM CLIFF — LONG LAKE — JORDAN'S POND — IDLING — A SHOWER — EAGLE LAKE — THE SNAKE STORY — BOATING WITHOUT OARS.

AKES like those of Mount Desert cannot fail to excite admiration. Beautiful in themselves, they give to the surrounding region as much as they receive. They are not all dignified by the name of lake, several being known simply as ponds. Three of these sparkling sheets of water lie on each side of Somes' Sound.

The most western is known as Seal Cove Pond. It lies on the north-east of Western Mountain and empties into Seal Cove. It is about four miles in length, and in its broadest part about a fourth of a mile in width. A dam at the lower end prevents the salt water from flowing in, while the fresh water does good service at the mill as it flows out. The ride from South-west Harbor to Seal Cove has many attractions. The distance is about five miles, and in reaching the lake it is necessary to go completely around the spur of Western Mountain. The cove was famous in former times as the resort of seals. At present it is a snug harbor for small craft, numbers of which are built here. At the head of the cove a high bridge is crossed, and, turning to the right, the lake comes in full view. At this place there are a few houses, yet the general appearance of things is rather sleepy. There is good fishing to be had, and trout and perch are usually ready for the hook. But we did not delay to test their appetite, nor even to row on the lake, as the clouds seemed to promise rain. The water looked somewhat dark, and around the shore the vegetation indicated that it was shallow, though in the central portions it is deep enough. At the head of the lake is a pond which serves as a sort of feeder. In passing on to Somesville we noticed but few dwellings, though we saw no less than two meeting-houses with their roofs falling in. Formerly they were occupied by Baptists, but on inquiry we learned that the religious interest formerly felt had greatly declined.

Before reaching Somesville, charming views were gained of the waters of the north shore of the island towards Trenton Bridge. The outlet of Long Lake was also seen as we passed. The water at this point runs toward the sound, and, owing to the operations of the mill, savored somewhat of the character of a saw-dust soup.

In going from Somesville to South-west Harbor on what is called the Pretty-marsh Road, we had a fine opportunity for observing Denning's Lake, which is about four miles long. For a couple of miles the road runs nearly along its shore, and the view is unobstructed by foliage. This lake boasts a single island. On the opposite side the long slope of Beech Mountain rises in its own peculiar beauty. As we go southward, the road gradually ascends along the base of Dog Mountain, while at the head of this lake Beech Mountain suddenly shoots up into the air, presenting that immense precipice known as Storm Cliff, and of which mention has already been made. In the brightest weather it wears a threatening aspect, and seems to frown. The wall of *debris* accumulated here at the foot of the cliff, descends rapidly to the deep water, which lies dark and sullen in the shade. This rampart of rock, lifting itself up into the sky, looks as if it would last forever, yet the unseen, but acting powers of the air are busily at work flinging down fragment on fragment, and the time may eventually come when the deep water on its front will not float a boat. The expression of the lake at this point is grand. Words cannot convey a just sense of its impressive character.

In visiting these two lakes we complete a circle, still leaving Long Lake, which lies between them, to be examined. The distance from South-west Harbor is about two and a half miles, by the Beech Mountain road, from which we finally diverge towards the westward, or left, and again at the proper distance, to the right. This lake is totally unlike, and has no connection with, the other two. It is situated in a long deep valley, or trough, between Beech and Western Mountains, which at the south end of the lake rises gracefully upward on either hand, like the inner side of a ship's walls, clothed with verdure to the top. We descend to its margin by a rough wood-road, gaining through the openings in the trees an occasional glimpse of the water, which, in a clear day, borrows its color, tone and expression from the skies; yet, at certain hours, the woody mountains photograph their green forms on its face.

The forest comes down to the edge of the water, except at the end, where there is a beautiful beach, drawn in the form of a bow, and covered with handsome granite pebbles. Here is found a lovely spot either for pic-nic occasions or solitary hours. The lake at this point is not broad, and a projecting spur denies an extensive view; yet this circumstance prepares the way for a pleasing surprise, when we get fairly launched in a boat. Descending the lake, the prospect opens until we look down the watery vista to the end. The beauty nowhere rises into grandeur, as at Denning's Lake, yet we find ourselves in a kind of picture-gallery, where an artist might profitably spend a week imbibing the pure lessons of nature.

When at Bar Harbor every person should improve the occasion to visit Eagle Lake and Jordan's Pond. The latter sheet of water may be reached from Southwest Harbor, by crossing Somes' Sound, and in going by this route a view may be had of Hadlock's Pond; yet most persons will find it quite as satisfactory to take their departure from the opposite side of the island, for the reason that this route requires the employment of only one mode of travel.

Hadlock's Pond has some attractions, being composed of two bodies of water connected by an apology for a creek, over which the road to North-east Harbor passes, but it does not demand a special visit. Jordan's Pond, however, will well repay the journey of about nine miles from Bar Harbor. The route lies by the way of Echo Notch and Otter Creek. About three miles beyond the latter place, the road to Jordan's touches the main road, turning back from it at a sharp angle, and running northward for the distance of a mile to the Jordan farm-house, which stands near the outlet of the lake. This is the only dwelling found here. Attached is a barn and some outbuildings that have felt the hand of time. The situation is solitary, but it is one of much beauty, and is capable of great improvement as a place of resort. A short walk through the fields terminates at the outlet of the lake, marked by a dam and the skeleton of a mill. The lake, for this is too fine a body of water to call a *pond*, is about two miles long, and about half a mile wide, lying between the southern spur of Sargent's Mountain and Pemetic, with the Bubble Mountains, or Twins, at its head. The eastern face of Sargent looks toward the lake, which, according to the fashion of these mountains, gives a long line of splendid cliffs, rising magnificently against the sky, a sort of Titanic wall. Pemetic looks across the lake at his neighbor, appearing grand and gray; while the Twins sit side side by side at the north, alike clad, as is meet, in robes of living green.

It was noon-tide when we reached the lake, where, among the rocks on the shore, the *cuisine* was set up and a fire put to crackling under a borrowed kettle, which was supported by a pine crotch. Amarinta pronounced the coffee prime; and when lunch was over we launched an old dory for the purpose of going on a voyage. But our plans were doomed to perish, for no sooner did the dory touch the lake than the water spurted up through a hundred holes. Thereupon Piscator cut a birch rod, produced his instruments of torture, and went off to inveigle the hapless trout. Disappearing among the bushes bordering the stream, he was seen no more until, in answer to our halloos, he left his rod and came forth to go home, having a string of fish in his hand for to-morrow's breakfast.

As for the rest of us, we lounged away the whole afternoon on the shore of the lake, saying, among other things, how fine it would be to push through the dense underwood skirting the feet of Sargent and scale the cliffs. We contented ourselves, however, with words.

It was interesting here to note the changes that

gradually took place on the lake. As the afternoon wore on and the slanting shadows were developing on the sides of the Twins, we found, as was also the case when we afterwards climbed them, that they did not stand side by side, but that one was pushed far in advance of the other, making out on the eastern side of the lake.

Towards six o'clock it began to grow damp and misty, and the fog gathered around the Twins, which caused one of the party to suggest that they were putting on their cloaks, preparatory to a general meet of the mountains. So we thought that we had better be going too. Therefore, after looking into the old farm-house, to see a man with only one leg, competing with the Lowell looms in the manufacture of cotton flannel, for weaving which he received ten cents a yard, we packed into our carriage,—an open one,—and drove off. Soon we had a pouring rain, with lightning and thunder, but Piscator drove up hill and down like mad, and brought us to Bar Harbor in less than two hours.

The last of the lakes to be mentioned is Eagle Lake, so called by Church, who sketched at Mount Desert during a number of summers. It stands higher above the sea than the other lakes, and is only two and a half miles from Bar Harbor. The outlet is found in a depression of the road half a mile beyond the foot of Green Mountain, and will be recognized by the frame of an old mill, which formerly made the water do some hard work. Of late years the mill interests in this region have been in a poor condition.

A short path through the bushes brings us to the shore of the lake, from whence the view up to its head is unobstructed. The lake in its general characteristics is bright and beautiful. It can hardly be said to possess the element of grandeur, under any circumstances, yet artists will perhaps find that it has more material for pictures than any other in the island. It is about two miles long, and of tolerable openness at the sides, while the country towards the north is sufficiently low to afford distant views of the nearest mainland. On the east side are the flanks of Green Mountain, sweeping gradually up towards the apex, and on the west is the low ridge running north from the sides of the Twins, while still farther west is seen the huge form of Sargent, its bold peak towering upward to the sky. At the south end the aspect of Pemetic is remarkably beautiful and bold. Starting near the east side of the lake, its ridge runs diagonally away towards the south-east, the top being sharp and rounded like the edge of an upturned hatchet. Without even a human being, the scene, especially when the lake is ruffled, seems full of life. So great is the variety, that even the solitary boatman seldom feels alone.

But as regards boats the lakes of Mount Desert are not particularly well provided, and it will often be found necessary to employ some wretched hulk, unless careful provision is made by an arrangement in advance. In the account of Bubble Mountain I spoke of rowing up the lake, but on another occasion I was not fortunate in securing a good boat, and Theologicus and myself were obliged to go up to Pemetic in an old leaky yawl, bedaubed with tar, with short pieces of board for oars. It was a beautiful afternoon, however, and a light breeze from the north favored us, so that we paddled thoughtlessly up the lake, not thinking how we should get back. As we passed the cliffs in the Bubble ridge, they seemed to come forward towards the water to look down upon us, and then gradually withdraw from sight. Towards the upper end they are between three and four hundred feet high, and crowned with plumes of pine. In one place the birches are so intermingled with the arbor vitæ, that it is impossible to go through without a sharp axe. At this end is a number of beautiful sand beaches, on one of which I found the track of deer. There are plenty of lake trout to be had, though of other kinds of fish there are none. I was here told of a great water-snake which formerly made its habitation in the lake. The story goes, that in a fire, which burned the woods, he was overtaken and broiled alive. I afterwards found that the story had travelled as far as Grand Menan, and the reader may be assured that it lost nothing in the passage. At that place I met a Lubec fisherman formerly acquainted with this

The Lake Region.

island. He was profoundly superstitious, and no marvel was too great for his faith. Everything in the shape of a wonderful story was seized with eagerness, and he would dwell upon ghosts with apparent delight. The people of New Brunswick were just then excited about the sea-serpent seen in Lake Utopia, the accounts of which, together with the preparations for his capture, filled several columns in the public journals. For my own part I was sceptical, and all the arguments of our friend the fisherman did not avail. Finally, a bright idea seemed to enter his mind, and he broke as follows:

"Say, now, ain't you from Mount Desert?"

"Yes."

"Wall, they had one *there*, any how."

"But that, according to the affidavit, sworn to in court, was seen fourteen miles away from the land."

"'Shaw, *that* ain't it. You've come all the way from Mount Desert and ain't heern tell on 'im. He wasn't *in* the sea. Now you know that mighty pooty pond up by Green Mountain?"

"Yes."

"Wall, that's the place where the sarpint was. He'd come right out of the pond and ketch a lamb an' eat 'im, and they couldn't do nothing, cos he was so big. But the woods got afire and killed 'im, and when they found 'im there wus forty jints of backbone a foot thick."

"Ah," was the somewhat incredulous rejoinder.

" Don't b'lieve it, hey? Wall, then, *I've seed 'em!*"

This triumphant declaration, made in a tone indicating the consciousness of victory, was accompanied by an emphatic slap on his knee with a hand nearly as broad as one of his own salt mackerel. Furthermore, I might see one of these bones myself at Bass Harbor, on my return. I, of course, promised so to do, at the same time putting down the name of the possessor of this remarkable but neglected relic, which would be sufficient to gladden the heart of Storer or Agassiz for a whole month.

But I forgot that Theologicus and myself were just now on Eagle Lake, that "mighty pooty pond," from which we did not escape so easily. Reaching the last sand-beach we climbed Pemetic. On looking around for water to quench our thirst, we found it was altogether unlike Homer's Ida, "abundant in springs," and were forced to accept a draft of lichen soup from a crevice in the rock. While here my mind recurred to a passage in Dr. Johnson's account of his tour to the western islands of Scotland. Being at one place by ease and choice, and with no immediate evil to fear, he nevertheless says, that "the imaginations excited by an unknown and untravelled wilderness, are not such as arise in the artificial solitude of parks and gardens,—a flattering notion of self-sufficiency, a placid indulgence of voluntary delusions, a secure expansion of the fancy, or a cool concentration of the mental powers. The phantoms that haunt a desert are want, and misery, and danger; the evils of dereliction rush upon the thoughts; man is made unwillingly acquainted with his own weakness, and meditation shows him how little he can sustain and how little he can perform." The force of these observations will always be felt by thoughtful minds when climbing among the slippery cliffs that look down in solemn grandeur upon the lakes of Mount Desert, but I hardly agree with him about the effect of such situations upon the fancy; for the unwieldy philosopher, treading like some elephant among the rocks of Mull, was timid, and therefore not qualified to stand, in this respect, as the representative man.

We lingered here until the mountain peaks around us were burnished by the rays of the setting sun, when we were favored with an unusually fine exhibition in the west, the rich golden glow being healthy in its tone, and altogether unlike those green-sick yellows which Bierstadt sometimes forces to the jaundice point.

At the last moment we began to stumble down the mountain amid the deepening twilight. This task occupied more than an hour. Finally we gained the boat, bailed her out, and, having no friendly breeze to carry us back, we were obliged to use our bits of board. These would have availed us nothing, if there had been a contrary wind. As it turned out, however, we had a beautiful, calm starlight night, and were able to paddle slowly down the lake. The echoes among the mountains on this occasion proved remarkably fine, the sound of our voices being returned from all quarters. So we cheerfully paddled on, only stopping occasionally to talk with the hills, or to bail out the boat which leaked like a sieve. In the course of the evening the moon rose from behind a cloud, and once looked out upon the lake. But gentle Luna seemed far from pleased with the prospect, and withdrew her face.

It was past ten o'clock when we approached the landing at the foot of the lake. At a little hut on the shore of a cove, a Harvard student and his friend were passing the night, in order to be on hand for the trout by daylight in the morning. We heard them singing college songs at the top of their voices, unconscious of the fact that they had an audience. In the afternoon they saw us paddling down the lake, but, not seeing us return, they concluded that we had left our boat and gone over the mountains. Unable, in the darkness, to find the landing, we hailed them, and in reply were invited ashore to the shanty, "to take something," "some hot coffee." But our heavy yawl was afoul of the sunken rocks, and we therefore declined their invitation, and requested a pilot instead. In a minute or two their little white boat, scarcely more than a skiff, shot out from the dark cove like a spectre, and after considerable trouble we were helped in to the only piece of beach found here among the boulders, and got ashore. Just then the moon burst out from among the clouds, flooding the pathway through the woods with a clear silver light. We accordingly bade our benefactors good night, and wearily began to plod the homeward way. At the distance of a mile and a half from Bar Harbor, we met the advance guard of an alarmed party coming out to the lake to search for us.

BEACH RAMBLES.

CHAPTER IX.

Marine Life — Sea Wall — The Ovens — The Gregoires — The Assyrian — Schooner Head — Spouting Horn — Great Head — Otter Creek.

EACH rambles at Mount Desert are invested with unusual interest, both by the splendid cliffs and caves, and by the immense tidal flow, which at the ebb lays bare the rocks and flats, unveiling a thousand secrets of the sea. Here the naturalist will find that a morning's walk is worth something. If really in earnest, he has only to step into a pair of long rubber boots, walk down to the shore, and, staff in hand, follow the receding waves. Among the rock-pools and shallows he will thus be able to explore the crystal dwellings of a large variety of marine creatures, and call upon, at their own homes, those marvels of ocean life that, farther south on the New England coast, might never be seen at all.

It is exceedingly interesting to inspect the huge star-fish and the monster anemone, whose outspread tentacles would fill a Derby hat; but, not everyone is willing to accept the invitation of the sea-side *savant*, who says, in the language of Caliban, "I prithee, let me bring thee where crabs grow." Most persons prefer to keep tolerably near the high water mark.

One of the most interesting localities for a beach ramble on the southern part of the island is at the Sea Wall, which is nothing less than the geologist's shingle beach. It appears almost as if built by human hands for a breakwater, a purpose that it indeed serves; and yet a Cyclop would be unequal to the task accomplished by the waves. From the Ocean House, opposite the steamboat wharf at Southwest Harbor, to the sea wall, is just a fair half-hour's walk by a good road. On this road, too, may be had some beautiful views of the entire mountain region that can hardly be surpassed anywhere on the island. Still, as we are supposed to be out for a *beach* ramble, it may prove as well to cross the fields to the shore. Here the prospect is also fine, the entire eastern group being in sight, while northward we look up Somes' Sound. The entire walk around to the Sea Wall is full of interest. The way is rough and liberally strewn with boulders, but the scene is animated, and the gossip with the fisher-folk on the shore is not without profit. The afternoon when I walked that way the weather was fine, the breeze mild, and only a light swell falling with a gentle lush upon the shore. The most of the boats had come in, and the men were cleaning fish, or mending their nets. Blue-eyed children were playing around the beach, some still waiting for their fathers to come ashore. The fisherman's life is a hard one, and his family suffer much anxiety, notwithstanding their familiarity with the sea. I noticed a young woman leading a couple of children and walking up and down the beach. Finally she went and sat on the bank, all the while looking earnestly seaward, straining her eyes to discover some object. She was waiting for her husband. Finally a well-known sail hove in sight around Cranberry Island, and came gliding on towards the beach, assisted by a leeward oar. When within hail, I heard her ask, "What luck, John?" The individual thus laconically addressed, and whose head was surmounted by an old battered "sou'wester," replied by going to the sheets and hauling part way out of the water a huge halibut that he was towing astern. The answer was satisfactory, at least so said the wife's face; and now, gentle reader, wish them ever good luck, for,

> "O well may the boatie row,
> And better may she speed,
> And muckle luck attend the boat
> That wins the barnie's bread."

As I went on I thought of the fisher-women of Venice, who go to the shore of the Adriatic and sing a melody until they hear the voices of their returning husbands chaunting a reply.

Coming around the point upon the south shore, the Sea Wall appeared in sight, a broad and high ridge, composed of loose boulders varying in size from a

Beach Rambles. 121

loaf of bread to a barrel, with the ocean rolling in on one side and a low meadow on the other. The material is thrown up in great confusion, and persons unaccustomed to such sights are invariably impressed by its magnitude. At this point the rock underlying the whole island is exposed to the ravages of the sea, which breaks off large blocks, tossing them in the surf until some great storm comes, when the fragments are driven up beyond the ordinary line of operation to lie at rest.

This place is somewhat celebrated for the fine specimens of green feldspar usually obtainable. The mineral occurs in masses of various sizes, distributed generally among the rocks. Specimens are valued as souvenirs of the island. It is of a beautiful hue, though possessing all the characteristics of the ordinary feldspar. But notwithstanding its friable nature it has been successfully worked in the manufacture of ornaments. This is an excellent place to collect sea-mosses. Opposite are the Cranberry Islands, on one of which is seen a church spire. Dead Man's Beach may also be seen. It is so called for the reason that, long ago, a whole ship's crew was drowned there and buried in one common grave. On the Sea Wall wrecks are not infrequent, and the bones of one vessel were still lying where they had been tossed above high water mark. There is little hope of a ship that gets nipped in this place, for she is tolerably sure of being ground to pieces.

There are other spots on this part of the island well worthy of being sought out, such, for instance, as Bass Harbor and the east side of Clark's Point. At the latter place a ramble may be had along the sound. Exploring in that vicinity one day, we found a hermit, who has lived for about ten years on the point of land opposite and close by Fernald's Point. He is of the same faith as the Jesuit Fathers who founded their Mission within a few rods of his hut in 1613, yet very unlike them in works. Hearing by accident of his existence, we resolved to pay him a visit, expecting to find one of those venerable characters seen in old pictures, with flowing robes, sandaled feet, and a snowy beard sweeping down his breast,

> "Like Barbarossa, who sits in his cave,
> Taciturn, sombre, sedate and grave."

But instead, he proved a short, red-faced individual, clad in a flannel shirt and patched, sordid trowsers, with the remnant of a greasy felt hat on his head. His house was a mere hut, about twenty feet square and eight feet high, the flat roof having just enough inclination to shed water. The only mode of ingress was through a latticed hen-coop, the roof of which was partially formed of an old boat turned bottom up. On invitation, we entered by this porch, and when the pupils of our eyes had accommodated themselves to the feeble light struggling in through a single pane of glass, the situation became apparent. Of floor there was none, save the mother earth. On one side was a bunk for sleeping, and in the corner a bin for potatoes, with an old broken stove in the middle. All was wretched and unclean to the last degree, yet he seemed to feel very comfortable. He was also in good spirits, having just received five dollars from an artist for sitting for his portrait.

A glance into the bin discovered a sitting hen spreading herself, as the hermit said, over a dozen and a half of eggs, while in the corner another venerable fowl clucked proudly in the midst of fourteen offspring that had just walked out of their shells. When we begged for a little more light on the subject, he drew back a shingle slide underneath the pane of glass and revealed a hole which he said was for the accommodation of his cat. Looking into a corner the eyes of Felis appeared flashing in the twilight like a couple of balls of green fire. Getting out again we sat down on a bench, and listened to the hermit as he told his manner of life, passed so democratically in his dingy den with his chickens and cat. He was weary of the world, and liked to be with himself. His summer work secured the winter's simple fare. What wood he wanted the sympathizing waves tossed up at his door, and as for candle he had none. The long evenings were specially consecrate to meditation, spiritual songs and prayer. All this was for the good of his soul.

Amarinta hinted that cleanliness was next to godliness, which sentiment gave this disciple of St. Francis so little concern, that it was followed up with a pointed homily on dirt. For this likewise the holy man did not seem to care either, and when bringing some water he still had the courage to present a cup which Amarinta vainly turned around once and again in the endeavor to find the clean side.

In striking contrast with his hut and person was his "garden," yclept a potato patch, without weeds, faultlessly neat, inclosed by a brushwood fence, and extending to the edge of the beach. From thence he volunteered to bring Amarinta a "nosegay," but finally presented only a sprig of mint, of which he planted a little for "sickness." Aureole, who is a judge, afterwards vowed it was for juleps, and cited in proof the hermit's red nose. We bade the hermit of Mount Desert good day, persuaded that we had at least found a character.

Still, the great beach rambles are to be had on the east and south-east sides of the island. Bar Harbor must be the starting-point for all those localities. To reach Bar Harbor by land from South-west Harbor, we first drive to Somesville, and then, turning the head of the Sound, continue on eight miles farther. For the greater part of the distance the road is hilly, and in some places exceedingly steep. The views gained on the road, however, are fine. One sight alone, the mountains seen from the Saddle of Sargent, three miles from Bar Harbor, will repay the journey.

The village of Bar Harbor, concerning which nothing in particular has yet been said, is beautifully situated within a short walk of the beach, and close to Newport and Green Mountains—here our ever-present companions. In front are the Porcupine Islands, lying in the mouth of Frenchman's Bay, and beyond are the Goldsborough Hills. The prospect is not altogether unlike that found in some places on the shore of Lake Winnepesauke, and we do not always realize that we are looking upon salt water, until we catch a glimpse of some craft peculiar to the sea.

A beach extends along the front of the village on both sides of the landing. Here is fine bathing for those who like the cool temperature of the water, while the geologist will be delighted by the glacial marks deeply cut on the surface of the rocks.

Bar Island is the nearest of the Porcupine group, and twice in every twenty-four hours the narrow strip of sand connecting it with the main is uncovered, as if for the convenience of visitors, who can thus, like the Israelites, walk dry-shod through the sea.

This place will be visited first by those who are resolutely bent on seeing the whole island; afterwards the "Ovens" claim attention.

The Ovens are situated about six or seven miles northward, and it would not be profitable to go the whole way following the line of the beach, on account of the difficulties that are met, and the projecting points of land that double the distance. Going by the beach it will be best to make Hull's Cove—two miles —the first point, taking Duck Brook Cove on the way. At high water a part of the way must be travelled along the rocks. In some places they are quite high and fringed with trees.

Hull's Cove is a very pretty place, shaped like a horse-shoe, and has a sandy beach. There are only a few houses. It was named after a brother of the General Hull who was *not* shot for his cowardice at Detroit, as the court decreed. Here dwelt Madame Marie Therese de Gregoire, a descendant of De la Motte Condillac.[1]

It appears that in the year 1688 the king of France gave to Condilkac a large tract of land on the main, together with the Island of Mount Desert, of which he took nominal possession, and executed several papers, in which he styled himself " Lord of Donaquee

(1)—In the petition of Madame Gregoire, her grandfather's name is spelled Condillac. Elsewhere he appears as " Antoine de la Mothe Cadillac, Lord of Bonaguat and Mount desert in Maine." He was a native of Gascony. In the Paris Document (N. York Col. Doc., Vol. ix. p. 594,) he is spoken of, under date of 1694, as " Sieur Delamotte-Cadillac, Captain of a detachment of Marines, a man of very distinguished merit." In 1694—7, he commanded at Michilimakinac. In 1701 he established Fort Ponchartrain, Detroit, remaining with his wife until 1706. The next year he returned to Quebec. In 1712 he was appointed Governor of Louisiana. In company with de Crozet, he controlled the trade and opened a silver mine. He returned to France, March 9, 1717; and it is said by du Pratz (*Histoire de la Louisiana*, Vol. i. p. 23,) that he died within two years afterwards. He is identified with the early history of five or six States. The Paris Documents, (N. York Col. Doc., Vol. ix. p. 446) say that he was well acquainted with the New England coast; but his connection with **Mount Desert was nominal.**

and Mount Desert." Donaquec was the Indian name of Union River, which empties into Blue Hill Bay. And in November of 1786, Madame Marie Therese de Gregoire, in company with her husband, Barthelemy de Gregoire, landed in this country from France, and appeared before the General Court at Boston, petitioning for the confirmation of her right, as the granddaughter of Condillac. In this course she was encouraged by Thomas Jefferson, La Fayette, and others. The court heard and granted her plea, July 6, 1787, and afterwards, by a special act, naturalized Madame and her husband, together with their children, Pierre, Nicholas and Marie.

In 1762 the General Court had granted the island to Governor Bernard, and the king had sanctioned the act, but his course during the revolution was obnoxious, and the island was forfeited. June 23, 1785, the court had also granted one-half of the island to Sir John Bernard, who had been friendly to the patriots; and the following December he agreed to pay two thousand five hundred pounds for the other half, but the contract was ultimately relinquished, and thus the Gregoires, as stated, obtained their rights. The vote, however, was intended to be a compliment to France, "to cultivate a mutual confidence and union between the subjects of His Most Christian Majesty and the citizens of this State.[1]

(1) — See Resolves of Mass., Vol. v. pp. 32, 131, 1789; Laws of Mass., Vol. i. p. 652, 1787; Papers Amer. Statistical Society, Vol. i. p. 76.

Madame Gregoire thus came into possession of about sixty thousand acres, embracing parts of the main land, and the entire island, except where already occupied by actual settlers.

On their advent at Mount Desert they began to sell off the land at a dollar an acre, but they do not appear, on the whole, to have been in very affluent circumstances. An old man at work in a field told me that he knew them well, and remembered the circumstances attending their death. Monsieur died first, after which Madame lived three years in the family of the Hulls, who occupied a house that stood on the site of the present brick one near the shore. After her death a belt full of gold was found on her body. About three-fourths of a mile back from the beach, the cellar of the Gregoire house is pointed out. Here, with their sea-side neighbors they lived a secluded life, dwelling upon the great memories of regal France. The old man, above referred to, said that they were occasionally visited by a French Friar; and that when Monsieur left home he usually went to lay in an equal stock of rum and molasses. Not, however, that he loved the sparkling vintages of Languedoc less, but Santa Cruz more. And too many of our sea-side friends are still overmatched by the same infirmity. At least the smugglers say so. At the cove, the antiquarian may give half an hour to digging among the Indian shell heaps, where perhaps he may find a stone hatchet.

Here it is best to leave the beach and follow the road until the burying ground is passed, and then strike across the fields of Point Levi to Saulsbury Cove. In going this way it will prove interesting to visit the graves of the Gregoires, found just outside of the burying-ground, at the south-east corner. We may rest assured that the Roman faith of the Gregoires had nothing to do with this exclusion. The grounds were laid out long after the Gregoires died, and, there being no monument, the graves were probably overlooked when the fence was put up. The interest that has been felt of late years in everything relating to Mount Desert has brought many visitors to the spot, now marked only by rude stones, but which, if we regard the interests of history alone, should at least be covered by a suitable monument.

The walk across Point Levi in a pleasant day is perfectly lovely. The woods and the fields are of the finest, while with what shall we compare the blue waters of Frenchman's Bay? The day we went to the Ovens the haymakers were at work, and the new-mown grass vied with the wild rose in delicious perfume, while the little folk we had along with us vied with one another in blackening their mouths with the ripe berries, afterwards pattering down to the cove, bearing long branches loaded with the fruit, like victorious palms.

Here we found our boatmen, who had come around

the point to meet us and carry us on by water, about two miles farther to the Ovens.

In going thither, always plan so as to reach the ground two hours after the ebb. The Ovens are nothing less than some fine caves in the cliffs which, being formed of a sort of porphyritic rock, is easily disintegrated by the frost and waves. The result is quite imposing. When the tide is part way down, a boat can be rowed under the largest. At low water a clean, beautiful pebbly beach is stretched along in front. The roofs and sides of the Ovens, when dripping with brine, present a variety of rich colors, combining with the rare lustre of the feldspar. The action of the weather is also slowly decomposing the surface of the rock all around on the top of the Ovens. A break in the cliffs affords a shelter for boats, and at the same time a place easy of ascent. Here come pic-nic parties innumerable.

South of the Ovens the cliffs are high and perpendicular. In a projecting spur is a long passage, through which it is deemed proper to pass. Some call it *Via Mala*, yet most persons are content to know it as The Hole in the Rock. Half-way up the cliff the harebells bloom in security, and here and there a miniature pine grows green in some rift.

A pleasant day here is always short, and the row back enables one to gain fresh views of the whole region that has been travelled on foot.

The next ramble should be southward to Cromwell's

Cove and the Assyrian's Head. The distance by the shore is perhaps a long mile, though by the road less. Starting from the steamboat landing, at low tide the whole distance can be done below high-water mark. Those interested in collecting pebbles will find some good ones, though there is nothing rare. Opposite Mr. Hardy's handsome cottage is an isolated rock. Every one must climb this, because, forsooth, it is Pulpit Rock. In some great cathedral, it would serve a good turn for the preacher. All along in this vicinity the schisty rocks are splitting up, showing signs of stratification, while huge boulders, brought hither by the Pre-Adamite drift, are seen struggling with the noisy surf. This ramble affords a fine view of the cliffs in one of the Porcupine Islands known as Wheeler's. The reason for the name now also appears, which is found in their resemblance to the back of the animal bearing that name. The likeness is not so apparent as formerly, for the reason that they have lost so many of their dead trees, which once stood as thick the quills of the "fretful porcupine."

At Cromwell's Cove there are fine studies in rock, but here on the shore further progress is impossible, the beach running down under the sea, which rolls in against a perpendicular wall. Getting at the right angle, a rock-man will readily be discovered, sitting on a pedestal half-way up the cliff. The peculiar cast of the features led to the name of "The Assyrian." He only needs a little more strength in his nose to appear a model man.

Near the Assyrian is a fine rift, forming a sort of cave, into which the sea squeezes itself with no little force and noise. An ascending path runs along the edge of the cliffs among the trees, affording an outlook upon the boiling waters below.

This ramble will consume a whole morning, and, in returning by the road, a turn through the fields near the Connor farm-house will afford a glimpse of the "Footprint" in a rock. I first heard of this through the medium of a magazine called *The Maine Light*, which lived through one number and then went out in darkness. The editor, in setting forth the attractions of Mount Desert, speaks of impressions of human feet found in the rocks here and in the neighboring isles. An inquiry among the inhabitants brought this to light. It has long been known as the Indian's Foot. It is about fourteen inches long and two deep, presenting what appears to be the impress of a very tolerable foot. It is, no doubt, nothing more than a very curious fracture in a metamorphic rock. Persons passing that way will of course go and see it. The children of the ilk will be glad to earn a dime in pointing out the exact spot.

In crossing the fields from the Indian's Foot to the road, that somewhat rare flower, the purple orchis, may be found on a piece of lowland. It is of peculiar interest, the reader will remember, from the fact that Darwin brings it in to help his theory of Original Selection, by proving the fructification of the orchis by insects.

Next in order is Schooner Head, three miles beyond the Assyrian. This must be reached by the road, as between these two points there is an unbroken granite wall rising up straight from the sea. The walk to Schooner Head, like all these walks, abounds with interest. It runs along the eastern side of Newport Mountain, whose hoary cliffs look down in such solemn grandeur, and comes out through a fine grove of birches to the head of a cove. Schooner Head is a noble cliff close by the entrance of this cove. It is probably not so high as the next headland northward, but all things combine to make it more attractive. It takes its name from the fact that on its sea-face there is a mass of white rock which, when viewed at the proper distance, presents the appearance of a small schooner. Indeed, there is a tradition that in the war of 1812 a British frigate sailing by, ran in and fired upon it, the captain thinking it was an American vessel. This is not at all unlikely, for one day when approaching the coast in a steamer, my attention was directed to that "little vessel sailing so close to the cliffs." This was at least a very good vindication of the name.

Here is to be found what is known as the Spouting Horn. It is a broad chasm in the cliff opening part way down to the water on the east, with a low archway on the south side at the bottom communicating with the sea. At low water there is a slippery and dangerous descent to the arch, through which it is possible to pass, and then climb fifty or sixty feet, escaping from this horrible place at the top. When the tide is rising, the waves drive in through the arch, with great fury; and in severe storms the force is such as to send up the water above the mouth, spouting like an Icelandic geyser.

This is a place where in climbing every one should move with the greatest caution; for woe to the hapless wight who slips when crawling through the dark and slimy arch. The boiling surf will suck him down into depths from whence he would never rise. The climb has its grim attractions, and young ladies even sometimes go through the Horn; yet most persons conclude that it is better to keep in a safe seat and watch the billowy sea.

A fine day is generally given to these rambles, but stormy weather is the best. At such times there is a wierd attraction about the sea-side. Button up your rubber coat, therefore, to the chin, tie on a tarpaulin, and go forth with your staff, breasting the storm. The investment will be found to pay. The lush of gently-falling waves is fine, but what is this compared with the sea in a storm, telling its angry thought to these mighty cliffs, and pouring all its wrath against their granite sides? The memory of such a day is enduring. Many an odd character is also met in these driving storms. Whichever way the gale may come it always sends such to the shore. Besides, there is ever a chance of a wreck, or at least of a hair-breadth escape. How fine is the spectacle of a ship struggling on a lee shore, and how terrible when it becomes apparent that Death is on board. Sometimes one may lend a helping hand, while often he finds himself in need of aid.

In the cove the fishermen have their boat-houses, and from thence that go forth to set their nets and trawls. At one of their huts was a shark's back-bone fourteen feet long, drying in the sun. Passing around this place, along southward of the cove, we come to the Mermaid's Cave, an enormous den formed by projecting ledges. Two or three hundred persons could here find room. At high water the waves go thundering in to its farthest recess. It is the truest cave on the island, and besides it contains the finest aquarium mortal ever beheld. Here is a wealth of anemones that Cræsus and Dives could not buy. They appear in all the richest hues in their rock-pool parlors, floored with a hard, limy substance, in color a delicate pink. Transferred to New York, it would prove of fabulous value. But this an institution that cannot flourish in the full light of day. It prospers best in the shady "caves and womby vaultages." Near the edge of the cave, where the sunlight strikes, the pools were without an inhabitant; yet where the light was properly adapted, the colony was numerous. Here these exquisite creatures, resembling some rare flower, live and die without moving from the spot to which they are attached. They do not seem to know any fear, and are as willing to be fed as a chicken, though when you put your finger in their cup-like mouths, they will fasten upon it with their tentacles. Their homes are exquisitely fitted up with a variety of delicately-fronded moss of all colors, with sea lettuce and pale green sponge.

It would prove unfortunate, however, to be caught here by the tide; and at the flood, as the waves come rolling towards the entrance, they often give a start, those who likened the cave to the home of Polyphemus now thinking that they

> "See Cyclops stalk from rock to rock,
> And tremble at their footsteps' shock."

Accordingly they leave its splendid pools and get out as fast as possible.

Our next ramble is to Great Head, the finest headland on the island, and the highest, it has been said, between Cape Cod and New Brunswick. It lies a short mile beyond Schooner Head, and is reached by the same road. Approaching the Head, we have a fine view of Newport's southern end descending to plunge into the sea. High up on the ledges are the nibbling sheep, foraging among the closely-cropped grass. Reaching the farm-house, most persons here leave their carriages, though the road extends some distance farther into the woods. The way is perfectly plain. The left-hand track leads by a gradual ascent directly to the Head. The woods are here and there largely sprinkled with fine old birches. Arriving at the highest point, a view is had far and wide of the grand old ocean, while landward rise the mountains.

This whole peninsula recently became the property of a Philadelphia family that has a taste for landed trifles. Among their effects, it is said, is an islet in Lake Superior, and a snow-peak in the Swiss Alps. But Great Head need not feel ashamed of itself in any company.

In one place there is a rough and steep descent nearly to the water, while in another a sheer wall leans forward, threateningly, over the sea. By descending the former a fine view of the face of the cliff is had; while a little way west, just below the gulch sprinkled with white rocks, is a cyclopean den called Stag Cave, from the resemblance to a stag which the imagination may easily conjure up when looking steadily upon some intrusions of milky quartz in the side of the wall.

Visitors are fond of coming to Great Head again and again to spend the whole day in sauntering from point to point, catching each new expression of the cliffs; or, book in hand, bestowing themselves under some convenient rock, to keep one eye on the stereotyped page and the other on the changeful deep.

Another fine ramble is to Otter Creek Cliffs on the ocean side of the tongue of land which makes the creek. The otter formerly abounded there, and hence the name. A separate journey can be made to this place by the way of Echo Notch, or else when at Great Head it may be reached by crossing the sandy beach on the west side. The specialty at Otter Creek is the cliffs, which are high, rugged and fine. There is moreover a cave called Thunder Cave. Following these cliffs down to the end, the creek may be crossed in a boat, and then come fresh beach rambles to North-east Harbor and the mouth of Somes' Sound, out of which, Agassiz says, when Mount Desert was "a miniature Spitzbergen," the "colossal icebergs" floated off into the Atlantic, "as they do now-a-days from Magdelena Bay."

Having reached this point in beach rambling it will perhaps hardly be profitable to return by the same route. It will be better to take the North-east Harbor road to Somesville, and thence, by the Mount Desert road return home.

FRENCHMAN'S BAY.

CHAPTER X.

D'AUBRI — THE PILLARS OF HERCULES — BOATING — THE ISLANDS — SHELL-HEAPS — ANTIQUITIES — MOOSE.

RENCHMAN'S Bay might perhaps be easily disposed of, by saying that here there *is* no Frenchman's Bay; and yet this would hardly prove a just proceeding. Besides, a multitude of witnesses who have loitered on its margin and tossed on its waves would rise up and declare me an imposter; yet, soft and fair, gentle Mount Deserter, for there is nevertheless somewhat to say.

The common story runs, as Williamson reports it in his History of Maine, that the name of Frenchman's Bay was given to these waters, for the reason that a French ecclesiastic, Nicholas d'Aubri, was lost here on an island. He refers to Sullivan, who tells the story with the important difference that he locates the scene on the west side of the Bay of Fundy, which Champlain says was named Frenchman's Bay by De Monts, though not on account of d'Aubri's adventure. This happened on Long Island, on the east side of the Bay of Fundy. At a[1] somewhat early date the original name appears to have been lost sight of. It was afterwards revived, and applied to the wrong place, the story of d'Aubri being imported to

---

(1) — Williamson, in his confused statement, refers for an authority to Sullivan, and Sullivan refers to Abbe Raynal and Cartier, neither of whom say anything about it. The Abbe (Vol. V. p. 344, Eng. Ed. 1798) simply mentions the fact that the present Bay of Fundy was first called Frenchman's Bay. In truth there is no authority for the notion that the bay received its name from the adventure of d'Aubri. Champlain in his Voyages (Paris Ed. 1613, pp. 13, 19) distinctly says that the bay was named by De Monts. He briefly mentions the affair of d'Aubri, but his language, as in the case of Lescarbot, shows that the bay was known as "*la grande baye Francoise,*" before the adventure took place. The account of d'Aubri has been so poorly stated, that it may be well here to give the version of Lescarbot, in the language of Erondelle, whose translation is now so rare:

"Hauing soiorned there some 12 or 13 daies, a strange accident hapned, such as I will tell you. There was a certain [Roman] Churchman of a good familie in Paris, that had a desire to performe the voyage with *Monsieur De Monts*, and that against the liking of his friends, who sent expressly to *Honfleur* to diuert him therof, and to bring him backe to Paris. The Ships lying at anker in the said Baye of *Saint Marie*, he put himselfe in company with some that went to sport themselues in the woods. It came to passe that hauing staied to drinke at a brooke, hee forgat there his sword and followed on his way with his companie: which when hee perceiued hee returned backe to seeke it: but hauing found it, forgetful from what part he came, and not considering whether he should go East or West, or otherwise (for there was no path) he took his way quite contrarie, turning his backe from his companie, and so long trauelled that he found himselfe at the seashoare, where no ships were to be seen (for they were at the other side of a nooke of land farre reaching into the sea). he imagined he was forsaken, and began to bewaile his fortune vpon a rocke. The night being come, euery one being retired, he is found wanting: hee was asked for of those who had beene in the woods, they report in what maner he departed from them, and that since they had no newes of him. Whereupon a Protestant was charged to

Frenchman's Bay. 141

Mount Desert at the same time. We might therefore be excused for saying that here there is, properly, no such thing as Frenchman's Bay. "Mount Desert Bay" would perhaps be a more fitting name. The statement of Sullivan that "there were, anciently,

haue killed him, because they quarrelled some times for matters of Religion. Finally, they sounded a trumpet throu the forest, they shot off the Canon diuers times, but in vaine: for the roaring of the Sea, stronger than all that, did expell backe the sound of the said Canons and trumpets. Two, three and foure daies passe, he appeareth not. In the meane while the time hastens to depart, so hauing taried so long that he was then held for dead, they weighed ankers to go further, and to see the depth of a bay that hath some 40 leagues lengta, and 14 (yea 18) of bredth, which was named *La Baye Francoise,* or the French Baye."

Thus the poor wretch was abandoned to his fate, and finally the ships went to St. Croix and prepared to spend the winter. But in the meanwhile Champlain was "sent backe to the Bay of Saint Mary with a Mine-finder that had been carried thither for to get some mines of siluer and Iron." And it is related that as they crossed the "French Baie, they entred into the said Baie of Saint *Marie,* by a narrow strait or passage, which is between the land of Port Royal and an Island called the Long Isle: where after some abode the said *Aubri* [the lost man] perceaved them and began with a feeble voice to call as loud as he could; and for to help his voice he advised himself to doe as *Ariadne* did heretofore to *Theseus,*

Candidaque imposui longæ velamina Virgæ,
Scilicet oblitos admonitur a mei.

For he put his handkercher, and his hat on a staues end, which made him better to be knowen. For as one of them heard the voice, and asked the rest of the companie, if it might be the said *Monsieur Aubri* they mocked & laughed at it. Bvt after they had spied the mouing of the handkercher and of the hat, then they began to think that it might be hee. And coming neere, they knew perfectly it was himselfe, and tooke him in their Barke with great joy and contentment the sixteenth day after he had lost himself."

many French settlements on that part of the bay, which is opposite to the banks of Mount Desert, as well as on the island itself," is a gratuitous assertion, which has no foundation in fact. The only ancient settlement of which we have any knowledge, was that of St. Savior, in 1613.

Still, what's in a name? If we were to send the name, "Frenchman's Bay," to the Bay of Fundy, where it belongs, these waters would not appear brighter nor the sky more blue. Therefore, while repudiating Williamson's stale story of d'Aubri, we we will take the present cognomen, *cum grano salis*, which is to say, with a little salt sprinkled on it.

Having now, as Mr. Oldstyle said, discharged "a duty to history," we may look about us and observe the characteristics of this body of water, which, in some respects, is finer than the waters around the outside of South-west Harbor.

Frenchman's Bay is about ten or twelve miles long and seven or eight wide. At its mouth is Schoodic Point, which rises as it retreats from the water, terminating in that barren peak known as Schoodic Mountain. According to the estimate of the Coast Survey it is four hundred and thirty-seven feet high. Its great compeer, Newport, stands opposite at the west side. Together they form the Pillars of Hercules at Mount Desert. Inside of Schoodic Point is Ironbound Island, while some distance to the north are the Goldsborough Mountains. Beyond is the town of Sullivan, and at the head of the bay is Trenton. Another reach of the bay extends in a northerly direction to receive the Skillings River, where at low tide there is a considerable fall. At high water a large vessel may safely descend, though not long since a schooner broke loose from above at about half-tide, and in shooting the fall rolled over and snapped off her masts. Towards the entrance of the bay, opposite Bar Harbor, lie the Porcupine Islands. Besides these there are no islands worth mentioning, except several that lie close to the eastern shore. Between Newport and Ironbound is the best fishing, while the sailing and boating are excellent everywhere.

Yachts of various sizes are always in readiness for a voyage, and every day they may be seen scudding to and fro. We frequently went in the Dolphin, a fine large sloop, with snowy sails, whose careful skipper had ploughed the deep for thirty years, and knew every inch of ground from Cape Cod to West Quoddy. With a stiff breeze it was a pleasure to see the Dolphin walk the water, bound, say, for the Ovens. In these little voyages we learned as much about the island as the bay, and at every hundred yards the former put on some new expression. A mile out from Bar Harbor it appeared in brave greenery, all the hills verdant to their summits, while up the bay towards the north, this character would gradually become lost, and finally in swinging around the shore the mountains themselves would disappear. It is, however, the more beautiful to bring them back again. At one point, near the Ovens, all that can be seen is the blue peak of Newport, but gradually the whole height comes forth, having a perfect pyramidal form. Then Green Mountain rises, and finally the distant ridge of Sargent comes in view; and when we sail in between Bar Island and Wheeler's Porcupine, Newport is no longer a blue filmy cloud, but appears before us in all its wild beauty.

There are many localities of especial interest around the bay. Each of the islands has some peculiar attraction. On Bar Island, already mentioned, may be had fine rambles and views of the mountains. The antiquarian can here find Indian shell-heaps that will repay the labor of investigation. From this place I brought away some arrow-heads dug out of the refuse of these aboriginal kitchens; also some teeth of the black bear, finely enamelled, together with part of the jaw. On the next island is an interesting fishing station, occupied in the summer by very intelligent and respectable people from Trenton. On the pretty little island adjoining, called the Thumb-Cap, is another station. Beyond is the Burnt Porcupine, while the last in the chain is the Great Porcupine. On this island, near the south side, there has been some search for Kidd's treasure in years past. The most delightful, however, to visit is Wheeler's. It is of great height, and affords the finest view of

Newport that is to be had from the bay, and which is a favorite view with artists. The cliffs in this island have often been sketched, and in the hands of a skilful painter are capable of great effect. Take a sunny day for a stroll here, and you will fix a picture in the memory that will endure.

Three or four years since a bear from the mainland swam over to this island, having a mind to try a little mutton. As it turned out, he did the sheep no harm ; for the people discovered what was going on and translated Bruin into steaks. At present there are no bears on Mount Desert, though a man at Bar Harbor assured me positively that one lately followed him on the road near Duck Brook.

In order to see the cliffs to the best advantage, it will be necessary to row under them in a small boat. This is perfectly safe, even with a heavy swell running, if you have command of the oars. And when out it will be well to visit the other island cliffs, if possible, as they possess features worth studying.

The cliffs on the sea-side of Iron-bound require a special voyage, and sails will be better than oars. The cliffs here, as cliffs, are superior to those on the shores of Mount Desert, though inaccessible to ramblers. On the same trip, if the wind is fair, many persons run across to Schooner Head and go home by the way of the shore cliffs, the interest of which never wearies. Approaching Cromwell's Cove, running close in, the Assyrian may be distinctly seen, though arriving in front he mysteriously vanishes, and appears to sink into the wall.

One of the pleasant trips is that to Goldsborough, by which we gain a somewhat near view of its commanding hills. Here is a pretty harbor which is most easily entered at high water. The village has a pleasant aspect, but looks down sleepily from the hill-side. The entrance of the Dolphin with flying colors, brought only a single individual down to quay, besides a couple of fishermen—one a Chief Justice—who had been spending a day looking after the trout. Their basket was so well filled with fine fish that one hardly need to fear recommending the waters of this vicinage to those who may be piscatorially inclined. At Goldsborough, however, the chief interest gathers around the shell-heaps, the relics of multitudinous dinners eaten during the old times by the Indians who dwelt around the harbor. These shell-heaps are often several feet deep, and sometimes cover acres of ground. They are mixed more or less with earth and ashes, and contain antiquities such as arrow-heads, stone hatchets and chisels, together with pieces of rude pottery, and the bones of birds and animals that were used as food. At the mouth of the harbor, the banks on either side are whitened by them. A sort of clam-rake with long teeth is the best thing to use in turning over the shells. In heaps like these may be found the bones of the moose, the deer and the bear, with those of birds. The smaller bones are sometimes worked into large needles or bodkins, of which the Indians often had need. These are all the memorials left by the once powerful race that ruled on these beautiful shores. Their arts were simple and few. In the Indian museums of New England, we find no sculptures to speak of that can be attributed to the Aborigines. I have seen on the handle of a pestle used to pound corn something that resembles the head of a snake, and in the collection at Harvard University, now being constantly added to by the zealous and well-directed labors of Professor Wyman, who has it in charge, there is a small image of stone. Perhaps this is the same that Whittier celebrates in one of his poems as a relic of the Northmen. This, with the exception of a fine amulet, carved in steatite, and found at Cape Cod, is the only sculpture of the human form that I have been able to trace to the natives on this part of the eastern coast.

Among the remains of birds found in the shell-heaps are a few of the bones of the Great Auk. One has recently been unearthed on this bay by Professor Wyman, to whom I am indebted for a sight of it. The Great Auk is now extinct, so far as these latitudes are concerned, and is only found in polar regions. There are now sixteen or eighteen specimens in European museums that must have been taken at a somewhat early date. The bones of the Auk tend to show that an arctic climate once prevailed here. At the same time the Esquimaux must also have extended down this coast. The Icelandic chronicles demonstrate, that in the eleventh century, a people called Skrællings, who possessed Esquimaux habits and characteristics, and sailed in skin-boats, were scattered along the shores of Massachusetts; and long ago they probably went northward in company with the Great Auk. We do not find any relics that can be distinctly attributed to them; yet occasionally the relics found even in these shell-heaps furnish hints of a people earlier than the Indians. Sewell, in his Ancient Dominion, is very positive, and after many investigations in connection with the heaps at Sagadahock and elsewhere on this coast, affording unusual relics, he says that the excavated rock-embedded kettle-bottoms "are the work of an earlier race than that which greeted Gosnold in these waters. These people," he adds, " were a sea-going people, skilled in navigating the deep in sailing vessels, sloop-rigged craft—and had vessels of copper for culinary use." What if these " sea-going people" were roving Northmen?

The bones most plenty in these heaps belong to the deer, but those of the moose are also found. We read in "A Brief Relation of the Discovery and Plantation of New England," bearing date of 1622, that in this new country there " is also a certain beast that the natives call a moose, he is as big bodied as an ox, headed like a fallow deer, with a broad palm, which he mues every year, as doth the deer, and neck like a red deer, with a short mane running down along

the reins of his back, his hair is long like an elk, but
esteemed to be better than that for the Saddler's use,
he hath likewise a great bunch hanging down under
his throat, and is of the color of the blacker sort of
fallow deer, his legs are long, and his feet as big as
the feet of our oxen, his tail is longer than the single
of the deer, and reacheth almost down to his huxens,
his skin maketh very good buff, and his flesh is excellent good food, which the natives use to jerkin and
keep all the year to serve their turn, and so proves
very serviceable for their use." After freeing his
mind of this leaden paragraph, the old writer goes on
to say: "There have been many of them seen in a
great island upon the coast, called by our people
Mount Mansell, [Mount Desert,] whither the Savages
go at certain seasons to hunt them; the manner
whereof is, by making of several fires; and setting
the country with people, to force them into the Sea,
to which they are naturally addicted, and then there
are others that attend them in their boats with bows
and weapons of several kinds, wherewith they slay
and take at their pleasure." The writer concludes
by declaring to his Royal Highness, Prince Charles,
to whom the "Relation" is dedicated, that "there is
hope that this kind of beasts may be made serviceable
for ordinary labor with art and industry."

Such are the glimpses of Indian life preserved in
the writings of that day. And in these shell-heaps are
the remnants of their feasts. Cobbet, in the course

of his winter's captivity, may often have shivered over the old hearth-stones that the antiquarian now digs out.

The most accessible heaps from Bar Harbor, are those on Bar Island and at Hull's Cove, and all of them require much patience and perseverance on the part of the digger, as the relics are not so plenty as some suppose; though in the cart-track at the former place I found a spot where the natives evidently made their arrows, as the half-shaped fragments were dug out all around it. The stone used was a variety now found near Katahdin, from whence some say it was brought. Going back to a period of three hundred years we may imagine that a village of Red-skins are here, and that still,

> "The old chief who never more
> May bend the bow or pull the oar,
> Smokes gravely in his wigwam door,
> Or slowly shapes with axe of stone,
> The arrow-head from flint and bone."

Yet this is only imagination. The old chief has gone forever.

FOG AND ITS EFFECTS.

CHAPTER XI.

The Air — Sunny France — The Gulf Stream — Fog — Leigh Hunt — Mist in Literature — Fog on the Mountains — Fog at Sea — The Phantom Ship.

OMPARATIVELY little has thus far been said about the atmosphere of Mount Desert. The most that has been written is the offspring of bright weather and fair skies. And yet there are two aspects of the case that should be considered in a candid estimate of the attractions of such a place.

The great Constable of France asks of the English,

"Is not their climate foggy, raw?"

Others have plied the same query regarding Mount Desert. The answer is readily given. The coast of Maine is not the Azores, nor Cuba, nor Bermuda. In the winter the air is "raw" enough to suit an Icelander; yet in summer the visitor who goes with tolerable lungs will find it bracing and agreeable. The Dog-days are an institution altogether unknown. At Mount Desert the Canicula exists only in the almanac. The shrilly-breathing zephyrus is always piping from the ocean for the refreshment of man, the mosquitos cannot live, except in the woods, and thin clothing is at a discount.

Still it cannot be said that there is always a perfectly clear sky. Tell it not in Gath, publish it not in the streets of some consumptive Askelon; but we must confess that in this isle, with all its enchantments, we find fog. Yet the reader should not receive a wrong impression from the above remark, since so much depends upon impressions. For instance, we all have an impression that France is " Sunny France;" hence it is not easy to make men regard what Bishop Cheverus said as true, namely, that they have as many pleasant days in New England in the course of a year as among the hills of Lorraine and Languedoc. Yet it is nevertheless so; and the reader is warned against the influence of any such formula as " Foggy Maine," lest it should prove impossible to demonstrate the fact that the summer climate of Mount Desert is equal to the attractive average claimed for the entire region by the genial Bishop.

The Gulf Stream, flowing out of the great tropic reservoir, ploughs northward in its ancient track, attended by a thin, invisible vapor, which, when it feels the cold breath of the Arctic Sea, is condensed like the steam from the spout of a teakettle, and rolls heavily away from the fishing Banks of Newfoundland in the form of confirmed fog, sometimes drenching every hill-top and valley along the coast. Mount Desert only gets its due share; and so far from being an objection, it adds to the beauty of the place, often throwing an ineffable mystery and charm over the entire island. Indeed, what would artists do without it? How well it hides a deformity or heightens an effect, let Landseer tell us in pictures of mountain scenery.

Whoever wishes to become an admirer of fog, should read Leigh Hunt's Essay. In his own charming way, he gives us the literature of the subject, showing the splendid use that Ossian makes of it, how Homer and Virgil introduce their gods and goddesses wreathed in its glories, and how Jupiter shrouded the Vale of Tempe with fog to hide his amour with Io.

It is to be confessed that Shakspeare was not in love with England's fog, yet Leigh Hunt goes into ecstacies over its effect when charged upon of an evening by the gaslight in London streets, an effect which he thinks worth mentioning in connection with the fine idea of Rhodius, who, after bewildering the Argonauts in the fog, brings down Apollo with his bow, in answer to their prayer, to shoot a guiding light before them to the nearest isle.

Here, and everywhere, it forms an element of sublimity, as well as of beauty. We had climbed one day to the top of Green Mountain to view the splendid panorama of land and sea offered to the eye,

"When suddainly a grosse fog overspread
With his dull vapor all that desert has,
And heaven's chearful face enveloped,
That all things one, and one as nothing was,
And this great universe seemed one confused mass."

I saw something similar to this once when looking down from Mount Washington into Tuckerman's Ravine, where the dense fog was tossed and rolled by fitful gusts, giving the appearance of a boiling ocean.

At Mount Desert we have an opportunity of studying every variety of foggy display. Some days, it is to be confessed, we found these vapory veils a sad annoyance. It was unpleasant when we had arranged the night previous for a tramp to Newport and a day of rare enjoyment, to look out of our windows in the morning and find that

"aloft on the mountains
Sea-fogs pitched their tents, and mists from the mighty Atlantic."

Our friend Aureole, who has already been frequently mentioned, and who occasionally indulged in a transcendentalism, told us on one occasion as we stood grumbling on the piazza, that our experience was not at all singular, as half the people in the world were in the fog all the time.

Yet in due season the advancing day often transmuted the cause of our wretchedness and discontent into pure poetry; and then, when tramping through Echo Notch, on the way to Jordan's Pond or Otter Creek, Choriambus would call us to

"Look down that dark ravine,
And watch the white and swittly-climbing mist,
Rolling in silence up the narrow fissure
Between those rugged, black, forbidding rocks,
Like troops of angels climbing fearlessly
Into a dark and rough and hardened soul;"

or else notify the less imaginative portion of the trampers of the all-important fact, that

> "From the hills
> White bridal veils of mist were lifted up
> By the gay sun, who kissed them till they blushed
> With light and joy,"—

a quotation particularly enjoyed by the young ladies.

We never failed to notice the fine illusions, nor neglect the mysterious antics played by the mist far out at sea. Here is where it is most effective in its exhibitions of magic. Sometimes, in a clear day, when not a sail can be seen in the whole offing, a great breath comes from the Grand Bank, spreading over the horizon a thin film of vapor, and suddenly a whole fleet appears sailing upon the sea. Whence come they? The philosopher tells us that a ray of light passing from a rare medium to a dense one, is bent downward; hence we always see the sun before he is really up. A slightly dissimilar operation of the light, reveals, perhaps, under favorable circumstances, a fleet of fishing vessels that is nearly out of sight below the horizon. Then with another puff of the breeze, the scene changes and this same fleet appears bravely sailing through the air. Again the fleet is doubled, one tier of vessels sailing over the other; or else, oddly enough, one tier bottom up, completely capsized—and yet securely sailing along the lower edge of a cloud, as the fly travels, feet upward, on a ceiling. At the Isles of Shoals this effect is witnessed oftener than at Mount Desert. Says Whittier:

> "Sometimes, in calms of closing day,
> They watched the spectral mirage play,
> Saw low, far islands, looming tall and nigh,
> And ships, with upturned keels, sail like a sea the sky."

As for the effect of fog upon islands, we had a splendid illustration of it in crossing from Grand Menan to Lubec, when the Wolf islands, lying in the mouth of the Bay of Fundy, and which ordinarily, from that point, appear as mere specks in the horizon, now lifted up their fine rugged cliffs far above the surface of the sea. In several cases the image was even trebled, so that three islands appeared one above another. As on the real island there were a number of projecting points, these, in the beautiful economy of optics, were elongated into huge Doric pillars, upon which the two upper isles seemed firmly planted, the pillars being displayed between like the columns of a double gallery. The sight was almost bewildering. The skipper said that he had often witnessed the same thing, but never saw a finer effect than this.

Leigh Hunt's admiration of London fog in the gaslight has been alluded to, and we may go back to the Isles of Shoals long enough to speak of a figure suggested in somewhat the same connection by Lowell, in a poem very unequal in its parts. The poem referred to is descriptive of White Island and the vicinity, and suggests the resemblance between the huge beams that dart from the lantern into the mist and the arms of a giant reaching up towards the tower from the waves. He says:

> "And whenever the whole weight of ocean is thrown
> Full and fair on White Island head,
> A great mist jotun you will see,
> Lifting himself up silently
> High and huge, o'er the lighthouse top,
> With hands of wavering mist outspread,
> Groping after the little tower
> That seems to shrink and shorten and cower,
> Till the monster's arms of a sudden drop,
> And silently and fruitlessly
> He sinks again into the sea."

Tennyson also makes a good use of mist, and illustrates its capacity for scenic effect. In the Idyls of the King, describing the departure of Arthur from the convent, from whence he was seen by Guinevere, the poet says:

> "And even as he turn'd; and more and more
> The moony vapor rolling round the King,
> Who seem'd the phantom of a Giant in it,
> Enwound him fold by fold, and made him gray
> And grayer till himself became as mist
> Before her, moving ghost-like to his doom."

A state of mind like that of the Queen's, would of course assist the illusion, yet both by sunlight and moonlight the effects of mist are often wierd and impressive in the highest degree, especially when they go so far in cheating our own senses. Hence comes the notion of the Flying Dutchman and the Phantom Ships in general, which find many a true believer among the old fishermen of Mount Desert. When the Phantom Ship is seen sailing up one of the harbors it is an evil omen. It means Death. She usually comes sweeping in under a cloud of canvass, yet with the silence of a ghost. As she nears the strand, familiar forms appear on the deck, while the master, like some immovable statue, points with his finger towards the sea. The old fisherman is perhaps about to hail, when a weird light flashes around her masts, which topple and fall, while the swelling sails fade into airy nothings. Soon, mast, sails, hull and all, are blent in ocean burial. The old fisherman starts, rubs his eyes, feels sad all day, and remembers it ever thereafter.

Whittier, who is so familiar with the coast, gives us a fine picture of these fog-built craft in his poem of the Dead Ship of Harpswell, to which, however, he denies a crew:

> "What flecks the outer gray beyond
>   The sundown's golden trail?
> The white flash of a sea-bird's wing,
>   Or gleam of slanting sail?
> Let young eyes watch from Neck and Point,
>   And sea-worn elders pray,—
> The ghost of what was once a ship
>   Is sailing up the bay?
>
> From gray sea-fog, from icy drift,
>   From peril and from pain,
> The home-bound fisher greets thy lights,
>   O hundred-harbored Maine!
> But many a keel shall seaward turn,
>   And many a sail outstand,
> When, tall and white, the Dead Ship looms
>   Against the dusk of land.

Fog and Its Effects.

She rounds the headland's bristling pines
    She threads the isle-set bay;
No spur of breeze can speed her on,
    Nor ebb of tide delay.
Old men still walk the Isle of Orr
    Who tell her date and name,
Old shipwrights sit in Freeport yards
    Who hewed her oaken frame.

What weary doom of baffled quest,
    Thou sad sea-ghost, is thine?
What makes thee in the haunts of home
    A wonder and a sign?
No foot is on thy silent deck,
    Upon thy helm no hand;
No ripple hath the soundless wind
    That smites thee from the land!

For never comes the ship to port
    Howe'er the breeze may be;
Just when she nears the waiting shore
    She drifts again to sea.
No tack ot sail nor turn of helm,
    Nor sheer of veering side;
Stern-fore she drives to sea and night
    Against the wind and tide.

In vain o'er Harpswell Neck the star
    Of evening guides her in;
In vain for her the lamps are lit
    Within thy tower, Seguin!
In vain the harbor-boat shall hail,
    In vain the pilot call;
No hand shall reef her spectral sail,
    Or let her anchor fall.

Shake, brown old wives, with dreary joy,
    Your gray-head hints of ill;
And, over sick-beds whispering low,
    Your prophecies fulfil.
Some home amid yon birchen trees
    Shall drape its door with woe;
And slowly where the Dead Ship sails,
    The burial boat shall row!

> From Wolf-Neck and from Flying-Point,
>   From island and from main,
> From sheltered cove and tided creek,
>   Shall glide the funeral train.
> The dead-boat with the bearers four.
>   The mourners at her stern,—
> And one shall go the silent way
>   Who shall no more return!
>
> And men shall sigh, and women weep,
>   Whose dear ones pale and pine,
> And sadly over sunset seas
>   Await the ghostly sign.
> They know not that its sails are filled
>   By pity's tender breath,
> Nor see the Angel at the helm
>   Who steers the Ship of Death!"

This, I believe, is quite an orthodox picture of the Phantom Ship, which still occasionally sails into these harbors, in foggy weather, to announce that some long missing vessel has been buried in the deep. To deny that the Phantom Ship was ever seen, would, in some quarters at least, be denounced as heresy. Besides, why need we doubt it? Sit on the rocks at Great Head and watch, and you may see one of these unsubstantial craft almost any day. Talking about this matter on one occasion among the cliffs at the abovementioned place, Mr. Oldstyle generalized the subject somewhat after the style of Aureole, telling us that it was not the fisherman alone who was led by phantoms; that life itself was one long *mirage* and full of unreal appearances shaped out of the fogs of the soul: while the ever-ready Choriambus chimed in with a Persian verse:

Fog and Its Effects.

> "From the mists of the Ocean of Truth in the skies,
> A *Mirage* in deluding reflections doth rise.
> There is naught but reality there to be seen,
> We have here but the lie of its vapory sheen."

As we rose up from our seat on the rocks, a strong breeze swept up from the south, dispelling all these weird illusions of the fog that hovered along the horizon, rolling away great fields of vapor, and leaving nothing before us but the open sea. Returning homeward, I heard Choriambus, who just then walked slightly apart, murmuring, half unconsciously, those well known lines from The Tempest:

> "These * * *
> * * * * * * *
> Are melted into air, into thin air;
> And, like the baseless fabric of this vision
> The cloud-capp'd towers, the gorgeous palaces,
> The solemn temples, the great globe itself;
> Yea, all which inherit, shall dissolve,
> And, like this insubstantial pageant faded,
> Leave not a rack behind."

FISH AND FISHER-FOLK.

CHAPTER XII.

EARLY FISHERIES — AQUARIA — JAPANESE LYRICS — WEIRS — PORPOISE — OIL — THE FISHERMAN'S LANGUAGE — HIS FAME.

CCORDING to the Mahometan theory, the earth itself is a fish; but, whatever may be our own views on the subject, we must assign to that order of creation a very large portion of its inhabitants. Fish form the fourth class of vertebrate animals, breathing through gills and travelling by means of their tails. Yet some fish, like those of Ceylon, would seem to view both of these appendages as superfluous, since they can live imbedded in the mud, or, like monkeys, climb the trees. The fish around Mount Desert, however, are of a very proper sort, and indulge in no such eccentricities, but follow the primal instinct, sporting exclusively in the sea.

The Northmen who sailed in these waters in the eleventh century, never attempted to utilize the vast stores of living wealth existing in the deep, yet no sooner had the existence of the continent been made known by the voyages of Cabot[1] and Columbus, than this whole coast swarmed with fishermen from the old world. But these fishermen were from Roman Catholic countries, while the self-willed, impetuous Northmen knew Christianity only by name and cared little for keeping the body under with abstinent fish. The season of Lent was nothing to them. But in order to supply the faithful on the continent with the duly prescribed food, the sailors of Biscay regularly sailed to these coasts, where, riding at anchor amidst the driving gales and drenching fog, they patiently hauled up the rich treasures of the deep.

We learn from Purchas and Hakluyt, that as early as the year 1527 a large fleet of fishing vessels, one of which was English, had assembled at St. John's, New Foundland, which was a place of general rendezvous at that time. Purchas also tells us of one old Basque fisherman, named Savelet, who at an early period had performed no less than forty annual voyages to these distant shores.

When the American colonies were established, the people were not slow to engage in the same profitable toil. Men of every grade in society were early interested, the noble as well as the humble born; so that the rhymster of that day might have said with truth,

"The Duke of Norfolk deals in malt,
The Douglas in red herrings."

(1) — Cabot is here mentioned first, in speaking of this part of the coast, for the reason that he had made more than one voyage to the continent of America before Columbus even saw it.

The people of Maine and Massachusetts were foremost in the business. The inhabitants of Mount Desert always enjoyed the greatest facilities for carrying on the fisheries, as the ground lay before their doors. And they know all about the work. Fuller said of Butler, the apiarist, that either he had told the bees things, or the bees had told him. The same might be said of these people and the fish. Yet there is *one* thing evidently not fully understood after all, at least by the fisherman, though possibly by the fish —namely, that the trade is overworked, or, otherwise, that there is too much fishing.

That is a dangerous theory which holds that there are just as many fish in the sea as ever came out of it. Acting on this idea, the fisherman is rapidly exterminating the denizens of the sea, as the hunter has already destroyed the game upon the land; and unless some wiser policy is adopted for the regulation of the fisheries, the cod may become as scarce as deer. On the English coast this fate has already overtaken the haddock. "Where are the haddocks?" said Mr. Bertram once to a New-Haven fisherman. "They are about all eaten up, sir," was his prompt reply. The shore races of this fish have disappeared, and they must now be sought afar in the deep water.

This contingency is not to be treated in an idle way, for if we refer to the condition of the fisheries two hundred years ago, it will be found that since then the quantity of fish in our own waters has fallen off in an alarming degree. Formerly a ship might be loaded with cod anywhere on this coast, while the very harbors were alive with whale and every species of the cetacean. Now to get a great "fare" of fish the dweller at Mount Desert must go a long voyage; while the hunted Leviathan leads his pursuer in the chase chiefly among the Arctic bergs. Also, on the British coast, where once eight hundred trawl hooks would take seven hundred and fifty fish, now a line baited with four thousand hooks will sometimes take less than one hundred. And if so much has been done to exterminate the fish in *two* centuries, what may not be done in *ten*? Long ago it was found necessary to protect the fish in our fresh lakes and mountain streams by the force of positive law; and with the great future of our country before us, a future whose necessities we cannot begin to estimate, even though restricted within the limits of a single century, who shall say that it may not soon be necessary to devise some wiser regulations for the protection of the inhabitants of the sea?

Yet there is a practical difficulty now existing in relation to the preservation of the sea fish. It is found in the fact that we know so little in regard to their habits. What for instance do we know of the most important of the food fishes, the cod? Next to nothing. We are even ignorant of the time when it begins to be reproductive. Yet how important is such knowledge, in view of its possible exhaustion and intelligent protection. Manifestly it is not for the interest of the fisherman to indulge in the present indiscriminate slaughter.

In other branches of natural history our knowledge is extremely full. Whoever takes up Mrs. Agassiz's work on the Radiates of Massachusetts Bay, will be astonished by the wonderful exactness of knowledge shown in relation to the origin, growth, and habits of this branch of the animal kingdom. The same knowledge in connection with our economic fishes would be worth untold sums of gold. This abundance of information, however, is readily explained by the fact that the habitats of the Radiates are all within reach, and subject to careful observation. Indeed, the parlor aquarium, which, when rightly managed, is a perfect miniature sea, affords ample opportunities for carrying on studies of this kind. On the other hand, we have no sufficient receptacle for the portly cod and the noble blue-fish and bass. Their home is in the deep, and until we have monster aquaria established along our coasts wherein these fish may thrive, and be at at the same time under observation, this branch of icthyology will make little progress. Would it not, therefore, be a wise act for our Government to establish such a depot on the North-Atlantic coast, where, by a course of exact scientific observation, the whole question of reproduction might come to be understood. At least this is the only way in which we can learn when it is profitable to kill fish and when to let them live. One writer says that he has the authority of a fisherman for stating that the cod do not grow at a greater rate than from eight to twelve ounces a year. He had seen a cod that was imprisoned by accident in a rock-pool on the shore, where he had the opportunity of observing his power of digestion for a period of several weeks, and found it weak, though there was an abundance of food. The haddock, he thought, would grow at a more rapid rate. And why could not every fisher-village, without waiting for the action of the government, establish an aquarium in some one of the many rock-pools that line this rugged coast? What village will lead the way and set the example?

In the care of the fisheries, the authorities of the Dominion are in advance of the States. For a considerable period trawl-fishing was prohibited by law at Grand Menan, and the act has now expired only by limitation. For three months in the year, during the spawning season, the capture of herring around the southern head of Grand Menan with nets is absolutely prohibited, and the officer in charge of this department often patrols the water on foggy nights, fully armed, to enforce the law. But at Mount Desert, as elsewhere on the entire coast, there is no restriction, and the fish are without a secure place to spawn. There are nets in the bay, nets in the cove, nets among the islands, and nets out at sea. These sea nets are of the largest class, and have as an auxilliary a good sized vessel and half a dozen men for a crew. One that I saw was over a thousand feet long and one hundred feet deep. It was managed on the bagging principle, the fish not being "meshed," that is, caught by the gills in the meshes, as their accumulated weight when dead would sink the net to the bottom, but were entrapped, as by means of a sack, which method leaves them still alive, and swimming freely, but fast prisoners. The meshnets are not more than a dozen feet deep, and are set by fishermen who generally live on the shore and among the islands, from whence they watch the approach of the fish, rippling in schools on the surface of the water. They can always tell when the fish are near, so that for a good portion of the time their nets are, of course, out of the water, which is extremely injurious to twine, and left to dry upon the shore. The nets thus exposed often reminded me of a lyric in a collection of Japanese odes recently brought out as curiosities in an English dress. There are quite a number referring to the sea and the fisheries. One runs:

> "By th' dim grey light of early dawn
> I strayed by Uji's wave,
> From whence the rifting mist upborne
> Me scattered glimpses gave
> Of Zeze's stakes there set,
> Whereon the fisher spreads his net."

Another expresses the longings of the Son of Udaisho Yoritomo, who became "Kubo," whatever that may mean,—in 1303. This individual, who was evidently so much dissatisfied with the city, exclaims:

> "O that throughout an endless life
> I might in peace dwell, far from strife!
> Forever watch the fishing yawl,
> And view the net's abundant haul:
>   How fair to me
>   How pleasant such a lot would be."

He would probably have joined very sympathizingly in the song of "The Jolly Jelly Fish," so often sung at Mount Desert.

But I will trouble the reader with one more of these lyrics, of the date of 1210, in which the hardships of the fisherman's life are set forth:

> "I would that I might show to thee
> The island-fisher's oft drenched sleeve,
> I would that thine own eyes might see
> How the salt waves their tints ne'er thieve;"

adding immediately, for this was a perfect Jeremiah among the "Japs":

> "From mine, alas!
> Aye, tear-bedewed, the colors pass."

There is even another still more destructive way of fishing. The net is fairly eclipsed by the weirs. These are huge traps, built on shallows and bars, in which the silly fish are impounded. Selecting some spot on the shore where the tide recedes at low water, a fence of wicker-work is made with strips of deal or spruce saplings, inclosing an area varying from one-half to three or four acres. A good-sized gateway is left for the fish to go in, and when once in they do not have wit enough to attempt to go out, at least in season, but go circling around the sides, shooting past the open gate. When the tide has gone nearly down, the fisherman enters the weir with a skiff, closes the entrance, and, taking a great scoop-net, jumps into the water and soon loads the boat with handsome herring, which are conveyed ashore to be put in pickle or hung up on sticks in the great curing-house whose smoke, in these parts, ascends forever. By this process the fish, both small and great, are alike destroyed. The small herring, indeed, have no direct commercial value, and should be carefully restored to the water as soon as taken, to perform their part in supplying the future stock; and yet these are all remorselessly thrown into the barrow and trundled off to manure the ground, which could easily be enriched by the inexhaustible supply of shells and other fertilizing matter now lying useless upon the shore. Gentle Islander, I pray you heed the voice of reason and common sense, and, while you slay your lambs at a tenderer age, let the young fish go.

One very earnest English writer says with truth:

"Our great farm, the sea, is free to all—too free; there is no seed, no manure to provide, and no rent to pay. Every adventurer who can procure a boat may go out and spoliate the shoals; he has no care for the growth or preservation of creatures which he has been taught to think inexhaustible. In one sense it is of no consequence to a fisherman that he catches codlings instead of cod; whatever size his fish may be, they yield him what he fishes for—money. What if all the herring he captures be crowded with spawn? What if they be virgin fish that have never added a quota to the general stock? That is all as nothing to the fisherman, as long as they bring him money. It is the same in all fisheries. Our free, unregulated fisheries are, in my humble opinion, a thorough mistake."

And disinterested, thinking men will everywhere be found to declare this judgment true; for only a savage will gather his corn indiscriminately, whether ripe or unripe, or cut down his trees to get their fruit: or, again, haul up his grass by the roots to make hay.

But while earnestly deploring this waste of wealth. it must be confessed that a visit to the fish-weirs is very instructive and entertaining. In some places the bottom of the weir at low water is left perfectly dry, as at Cape Cod, where the fisherman has only to walk in and pick up the blue fish on the sand; and in others, as at Lubec and Campo Bello. there is always water enough for a whale. At Lubec I saw the remains of a shark caught thus, that was about thirty feet long, and whose liver made five barrels of oil. Sometimes they are taken there forty feet in length. In such cases they make a formidable fight, and the trusty rifle must come in as the auxiliary of the harpoon. At Mount Desert they occasionally find a good-sized shark or horse mackerel. but oftener the porpoise thus comes into the weir. Schools of these continually gambol about the bay for the edification of visitors, or as a prize for the Indians who hunt them for oil. I started once across Frenchman's Bay for their camp on Iron-bound Island. to see them at home, paddling with an old trapper in his bark canoe; but when we got halfway over, a hard rain-storm set in, and we thought it best to return at once. Still the trip afforded an opportunity of testing the qualities of the "bark" on the long ocean swell. No boat could have behaved more admirably. But to return.

Sometimes the porpoises show their glittering backs close in by the quay. and seem on the point of landing for the purpose of applying for rooms. Contrary to the views of many persons. the porpoise *(Phocœna communis)* is not a fish at all, having only a few of the eccentricities of the fish, and living in the water, forming a curious connection between the two most distant orders of Vertebrates, the mammalia being the highest and the fish the lowest. Some say that it *looks* like a fish, and *lives* like a fish, and that to all intents and purposes it *is* a fish; yet if the porpoise is a fish, Izaak Walton was a fish; whereas, in truth, he was simply a fisherman. In its most distinguished feature, the porpoise is more a *man* than a *fish*. Like the Pearl-diver, he is constantly diving; yet whatever he does, unlike a fish, he must come to the surface and breathe. The difference between the diver and the porpoise is, that the latter can hold his breath longer than the former. The porpoise can carry an extra supply of air. So a man going down in a diving-bell carries a little atmosphere around him, but the porpoise's diving-bell is *within* him. Thus much for the porpoise.

When visiting the weir at Bar Island, we were not favored by an interview with this creature, yet a numerous assemblage of the finny tribes awaited inspection.

The fisherman in charge was very accommodating, and ferried Amarinta and the rest over the shallow water into the weir, and then waded in with his scoop-net and proceeded to catch the herring, which rushed about the weir exceedingly frightened. When dropped out of the net into the boat, they set up a prodigious drumming. The herring in the water could be distinctly seen, their sides flashing like silver. The rest of the fish did not seem to mind our presence, and swam leisurely around the boat, or lay still while we paddled among them. Besides the herring there were menhaden, silvery hake, dog-fish, rockcod, sculpin, flounders, pollock, scates, and goose or monkfish. The two latter were extremely tame, and several of the monk-fish were five and six feet long. Putting the blade of an oar into its broad mouth, this fish would hold on with its teeth until drawn up to the boat, and when alongside they would swim slowly, so that we could touch their backs with our hands. In the water, their movements are as dignified as those of an empress dragging a long train. On the other hand the scate is rather clumsy, and when I tipped them over on their backs, they had hard work to recover from this position. Such a multitude of fish, for there were thousands of them, all at home in their native element, formed a rare sight, and one for which the naturalist might well afford a journey to Mount Desert.

Cod are not taken in these weirs, but are fished with lines and trawls. This is called boat-fishing Fishing with lines is very laborious work, as it often occupies the whole night, some fish being taken only at that time. Trawling, however, is more easy. By this method the fisherman fastens a hundred or two baited hooks at regular distances on a small rope, which is sunk to the bottom and left, each end being marked by a buoy to which they are attached. The fisherman leaves it to itself, and only goes at certain hours to rebait the hooks and take off the fish that are caught. This practice is very destructive, and should be suppressed by law; that is, unless we wish to banish the cod and the haddock to deep water.

Some of the fishermen talk very sensibly on this and other subjects connected with the fisheries. It was quite entertaining to go on board of their vessels as they lay in the harbor, and enter upon conversation. I found two distinct classes of fishermen, that may be called the old school and the new. The former are open to suggestions, and anxious to profit from science, while the latter kept old horse-shoes nailed to the foremast, near the deck, to drive away the witches, and think that there is no danger of exhausting the supply of fish. There were "fish enough" in the sea. "But why don't you catch them?" I inquired. "Well, they didn't know; the people threw so much 'gurry' overboard in the harbors." By this they meant the heads and entrails of the fish. They seemed to think that it had something of the effect of pirates hung on headlands in chains, or the grinning skulls of bold highwaymen, fixed on spikes over London gate. Once, as they confessed, it was easy to go off in a boat and get fifteen dollars' worth of hake in a few hours, but now they often toiled all the night and took nothing. They did not however throw away all the "gurry." The liver and the sounds, that is, the air vessels attached to the back-bone, are carefully preserved, the livers for oil, and the hake sounds for sizing. and—would you believe it, lads and lasses?—for gum-drops. It is nevertheless so, and when at the confectioner's you roll the unhealthy things under your tongue, as a sweet morsel, dreaming of the Asiatic Acacia bleeding away its rich life in a thick resinous ooze. just remember that *your* gum may have originated in the fish-tubs of Mount Desert.

Those interested in cod liver oil will also perhaps feel unwilling to learn that this thing can seldom be had. There are doubtless persons who manufacture it, and I could readily point at least to one—yet careful observations extending along the Maine coast from Isles of Shoals to Grand Menan, did not afford me a glimpse of a gallon of the genuine stuff. The most of the fishermen frankly acknowledged that everything in the shape of a liver went into the common vat; while others confessed the truth when it was urged home. Let consumptives take notice.

Still there is no moral obliquity on the part of the fisherman. He simply sells the livers at so much the bucket to the factor or speculator, and usually speaks of the product as "liver oil." If speculators call this stuff "cod liver oil," when they put it in the market, it certainly is not his fault. The fisherman himself is generally a good-hearted man, notwithstanding his rough exterior, and in many cases maintains a noble independence. He will do the sea-side visitor a service, and, notwithstanding his poverty, decline receiving any remuneration. These cases are all the more noticeable, for the reason that most of the people by the sea-side, feel that the summer is their harvest-time, and that they must hasten to make as much out of strangers as they can.

The fisherman's home is not always so comfortable as I could wish, yet he does not always seem to feel *that*. He is used to roughing it. And, like the gipsy, he has a language of his own. On the whole, his is a queer vocabulary.

Speaking of "brush," he means his hair. His boots are "stompers;" one knife is "throater," and the other a "splitter;" his apron is a "barvel," his fish-box is a "kid;" his hook is a "dragon;" his hand-net is a "dipper," and most all small craft are "pinkies," or "pogies," "smacks," or "jiggers." He counts time by the tide; he was married at about "slack water." He reckons the length of his lines by "shots," thirty fathoms to a shot; the principal preparations of food containing flour or meal, are known as "fresh smother," "duff," and "jo-floggers," while hard-bread and apples is "grunt." Going out to take a walk forms a "cruise," and when he leaves a neighbor's fireside to go home, he gets "up anchor" or "killick." A breath of wind on the water is a "cat's-paw," and everything is called "she," from his wife, that is "my old woman," to a cart-wheel or a clock.

The accessories of the fisherman's vocation may appear rude, but his calling is closely connected with the most important interest. It has also been followed by those who have invested it with a sort of dignity. First of all, the Apostles were chiefly fishermen, and the Pope himself is not ashamed in this our own day to carry in his pocket the annual revenues of his eel fisheries at Comacchio. And all along the centuries the fisherman has made himself felt. In 1750, the Fishmongers' Company, the oldest in the English realm, in addressing the Prince of Wales, told his Highness that the Company had furnished London three-score Lord Mayors. Venice rose from a fishing village, and Amsterdam was founded on herring-bones. Phipps and Pepperell were in the business, and both were knighted. John Selman and Nicholas Broughton, Marblehead fishermen, were the first naval commanders appointed by Washington, while Commodore Tucker, the fisherman, took more British guns than the famous Paul Jones. Their record has always been honorable, and a generous people will ever accord them all praise.

THE ISLES OF SHOALS.

CHAPTER XIII.

JOHN SMITH — CHAMPLAIN — HISTORY OF THE ISLES — APPLEDORE — LONDONNER'S — WHITE ISLAND — STAR — SMUTTY-NOSE — ROCKWEEDS.

ORTSMOUTH, the point of departure for the Isles of Shoals, is a quaint old place of some historic renown, situated at the mouth of the Piscataqua River. From thence, in the summer season, a small steamer usually makes a daily trip to the Shoals. It was our fortune, however, to sail thither in the little yacht *Celia*. As the tide was unfavorable, the Captain had left his vessel at Newcastle, about a mile below, and brought up his yawl to take us down. On such a perverse stream as this, the task of rowing is no trifle, yet after a hard struggle, in which the tide at times got the best of us, tugging at the bows of the boat like some huge mastiff, we got down the harbor, passing on the way mementos of at least three wars.

Getting on board just as a heavy shower came on, blistering the surface of the water, we at once went below, though the crew got the yacht under way; and when the shower was over, the Celia was outside of

Portsmouth Light. We were now heading directly for the "Shoals," as the people here say, with Whale Back Light to our left, or larboard side. This beacon has a fixed light in a solid tower, fifty-eight feet high, built upon a small rock.

Gradually Appledore rose above the waves, until it seemed to float insensibly

"Like a great ship at anchor."

As we sailed on, it became evident that we were approaching

"A country that draws fifty feet of water,
In which men live as in the hold of nature.
   *   *   *   *   *
A land that rides at anchor, and is moored,
In which they do not live but go aboard."

Or, if any one does not exactly like this figure,

"That live as if they had been run aground,"

for I should hardly care to carry out Butler's description of Holland any farther. Arriving off the cove on the south side of Appledore, it was pleasing to find the aspect of these isles so agreeable. Instead of a mere heap of black, unsightly rocks as I had anticipated, the colors were rich, cheerful and harmonious; and, being half covered here and there with bright green shrubs, the effect of the islands, as a whole, when laid against the bright blue sky, was really admirable. I should have been glad if I could have said at once with Caliban, "This island's mine."

Going ashore seemed like going out of the little steam tug to get on board the Great Eastern. Yet we soon found the difference, for instead of a reeling deck there was the solidity of *terra firma*. We therefore concluded that Butler's last suggestion was best, and that the whole concern had run hard aground. But what is the genealogy of these isles?

That class of writers who scorn investigation, and seize upon the first plausible story that they can conveniently catch, have been accustomed to say that the Isles of Shoals were discovered in 1614, by Captain John Smith, who drew " the first map of this coast." Now, as regards John Smith, the simple truth is, that in the above-mentioned year he came to the coast of Maine, and left his vessel at Monhegan, " Whilest," as he says, " the sailors fished, myselfe with eight others of them might best be spared, ranging the coast in a small boat." In the course of this voyage he drew a map, and laid down these isles as " Smith's Isles." There is not, however, a line on record to prove that he ever stepped upon their shores.

Such is the claim of John Smith as the " Discoverer" of the Isles of Shoals, so familiar to fishermen and others who had already frequented the coast for many years.

In this connection Champlain must be noticed. With De Monts, he explored this region in 1605, nine years before Smith arrived, and made a map of the coast. This is the first tolerable map to which we can refer. Lescarbot says that they "explored many things," "viewing all the coast of this land," and "searching to the bottom of the bays."

Champlain approached this part of the coast May 15. At the east he saw three or four isles, and at the west the mouth of a bay, that is, Portsmouth harbor, whose islands he mentioned as covered with wood. He afterwards landed at Odiorne's Point, which he laid down in his map and called Cape of the Isles (*Le Cap aux isles*). Therefore, if either of these explorers should be distinguished as the discoverer of the isles, the honor must be awarded to Champlain.

In regard to the origin of their present name we are left in doubt. It has often been said that it superseded the name given by the founder of Virginia, who called them "Smith's Isles," yet this is a gratuitous assumption. There is nothing to prove that the name "Isles of Shoals" did not *precede* Smith's name. No one ever spoke of "Smith's Isles," except Smith himself; whereas it is not known when they were first called the "Isles of Shoals." The name was doubtless given by some fishing expedition, on account of the schooling of the fish at this place, and perhaps by Sir Samuel Argall, who, the year previous to the arrival of Smith, fished in these waters.

But though the origin of the name may be obscure, there is no doubt but that they were settled at a comparatively early period. Lovett said: "The first place I set my foote vpon in New England [1623] was the Iles of Shoulds * * * Vpon these Islands I neither could see one good timber tree, nor so much good ground as to make a garden." He adds that this is good fishing ground for "6 Shippes," but not more, owing to the lack of stage-room. The fact was demonstrated, he says, by "this yeare's experience." Thus early were the New Englanders found here.

The isles are seven in number, lying nine miles south-east of Portsmouth Light. The line dividing Maine from New Hampshire passes through them, leaving Appledore, Haley's, now called Smutty-nose, Duck and Cedar Islands in the former State; and Gosport or Star Island, White and Londoner's Island in the latter. The largest is Appledore. Star Island ranks next, and Haley's stands third. The others are hardly more than rocks.

The name of the first settler is not definitely known, though it might have been that Jaffrey, who, in 1628, with a Mr. Burslem, paid part of the expense of arresting Thomas Morton, of Merry Mount. Morton himself was brought here at that time, previous to being sent to England.

In 1635 the southern half of the group was granted to John Mason; but in 1676 the isles were occupied by William Pepperell (father of Sir William) and a Mr. Gibbons. They engaged for a time in the fisheries, but finally decided to remove.

We read that the Northmen, when they went into

Iceland, were guided in the choice of ground for their colonies by the hints thrown out by the seat-posts, which, being carved with images of the gods, they threw overboard when approaching the coast, to land where the winds and waves might toss them. But Pepperell and his associate were guided by a simpler suggestion. They cared nothing for Lares and Penates, and therefore each took a stick, set it on end, and allowed it to fall as it would, then going to seek new stations in the direction indicated by the fallen sticks. Pepperell's fell to the north-west, and sent him to Kittery, while Gibbons' guided him to the Waldo Patent. At least, so says *tradition*.

It is also stated, on somewhat better authority, that Sir William's father was so poor, that for some time after his arrival in this country he sought a wife in vain. When he became more prosperous, the damsel of his choice became his wife. Their son was knighted for his services in 1759. The title became extinct in 1816, and it is said that those who bore it actually came to want. Margery, a sister of Sir William, was accidentally drowned near the isles.

August 14, 1636, Richard Mather, grandfather of the celebrated Cotton Mather, arrived from Bristol, England, in the James, commanded by Captain Taylor. In his journal Mather says, " But ys evening by moone-light about 10 of ye clocke wee came to anere at ye Iles of Shoals, which are 7 or 8 Islands and other great rockes; and there slept sweetely yt night till breake of day. But yet ye Lord had not done with us, nor yet had let us see all his goodnesse which he would have us take knowledge of; therefore on Saturday morning about breake of day, ye Lord sent forth a most terrible storme of raine and easterly wind, whereby wee were in as much danger as I thinke ever people were: for we lost in yt morning three great ancres and cables; of which cables, one having cost 50£ never had beene in any water before, two were broken by ye violence of ye waves, and ye third cut by ye seamen * * to save ye ship." Then they set sail, "but ye Lord let us see yt sayles could not save us, * * for by ye force of ye wind and raine ye sayles were rent in sunder." Then he says they began "to drive with full force of wind and rayne directly upon a mighty rocke standing out in sight above ye water, so yt we did but continually wayte when we should heare and feele ye dolefull rushing and crushing of ye ship upon ye rocke." But happily the ship was guided past "ye rocke" and escaped, when new sails were bent on, and the James headed in safety for Cape Ann. The same storm cast another emigrant ship ashore at Cape Ann, where twenty-one persons were drowned, including Mr. Mather's brother-clergyman, Mr. Avery, from Wiltshire, and his wife and six children.

About this time the trade of the isles was quite flourishing, and as many as half-a-dozen ships would be loading with fish for Bilboa, in Spain. The inhabitants were poor, but distinguished for genuine worth.

In 1646, one John Abbot, who had been taken prisoner by the Indians at Black Point, managed to escape with a pinnace of thirty tons, and came to the Isles. On a favorable occasion, when the Indians were ashore, he greased the mast, hoisted the sail, and was soon beyond their reach.

At first the isles were left without any settled government, but the inconvenience became so great, that in the year 1661, Massachusetts erected them into a township, one part lying in the county of York and the other part in that of Dover and Portsmouth, under the name of "Apledoore;" though, by a subsequent act in 1672, they were all placed in the jurisdiction of Dover. The first settlement was on Appledore, then known as Hog Island. The number of inhabitants at that time has always been exaggerated. It is clear that the number of dwellings did not exceed twenty. They had a small meeting-house. It is *said* that the Rev. Mr. Hull was the first preacher, though Savage shows that he was here not long before his death in 1665. The inventory of his widow states that the "the Isle owed him for his ministry £20." Richard Gibson, of the Church of England, came here, "entertained by the fishermen" to preach to them. He also, as John Winthrop complains, "did marry and baptize." To this he added the crime of speaking against the Great and General Court, saying that the Shoals were not within their jurisdiction. Being apprehended by the Boston authorities, he acknowledged his guiltiness (in their eyes), and, "being a stranger," was graciously sentenced "to depart the country," without any "other punishment." He left for England in 1642.

Appledore was early abandoned, the people removing to the convenient location afforded by Star and Haley's Island. On the latter was a building that served as a Court House, and, in 1672, cases involving not more than ten pounds could be tried here, "Provided one person or more from the mayne do sitt and joyne with them." At the same time dues of gunpowder could be collected of vessels entering the port, which powder should be used for "our safety."

Two years previous to this time, however, the isles came near losing their good name, and bringing "reproach and prejudice to this colony;" for it was reported to the General Court, "that there is a ship riding in a roade at the Isles of Shoals suspected to be a pirat, and hath pirattically seized the say'd ship and goods from some of the French nation in amity with the English." The virtuous Court, therefore, thought fit to purge itself of all complicity with the affair, and its resolve, to that effect, as the record quaintly says, was duly "Publisht in Boston by beat of drume."

The people here were in no way implicated, and yet we find that the first pirates in New England originated near by, beginning their depredations in

1632, and generally keeping east of the Shoals. They were sixteen in number, being led by Dixy Bull. Pemaquid was their first prize, and there one of their band was killed. The Government sent an armed vessel in pursuit of them, but, on their promising to abandon the trade, the chase was given up. It is said that they had one rule against excessive drinking, and another enforcing daily prayers. Sometime afterwards the Low Pirates visited the isles and caused one of the fishermen to purchase his life by cursing the renowned Cotton Mather three times. They hated the Reverend gentleman not without cause, for he really seemed to enjoy preaching a sermon at the execution of one of their profession.

December 24, 1715, the present town of Gosport was erected by the authorities of New Hampshire, the old jurisdiction of "Apledoore" having become effete. In 1728 Gosport's proportion of the tax of one thousand pounds was sixteen pounds four shillings.

The present records go back no farther than the year 1730, but they contain much interesting information both of a civil and ecclesiastical nature.

It appears that in the year 1647, it was contrary to the orders of the General Court for a woman to live on the isles, and a man was complained of for bringing over some goats and hogs, together with his *wife*. The hogs preyed upon the fish which was being cured, but the crime of the poor woman is not mentioned. To the credit of the judges we must add, that while the porkers were banished the isles, the man was allowed to enjoy the companionship of his wife. The minister from 1651 to 1663 was the Rev. John Brock, a graduate of Harvard College, who appears to have been a man of great excellence. Cotton Mather tells a good story about him in his *Magnalia*. He says that a fisherman who had been very useful in ferrying the people to church on Sundays, finally lost his boat in a storm. The good parson, hearing him lament the fact, said, " Go home contented, good Sir, *I'll mention the matter to the Lord;* to-morrow you may expect to find your boat." And the account says that the next day it was actually restored to him, having been brought up from the bottom on the flukes of an anchor. Mr. Brock was succeeded by a Mr. Belcher. Afterwards the Rev. Joshua Moody took the clerical duties, and served from 1706 to 1731.

The Rev. John Tucke was the minister from 1732 until 1773. At first his salary was one hundred and ten "pounds money or bills of credit," to which was added five pounds towards a house. He accepted the office April 28, and July 26 following was observed by the inhabitants as a day of fasting and prayer for a blessing on his ministry. In 1754 his salary was one quintal of "merchantable fish" to each man, and his parishioners numbering nearly one hundred, his stipend, for those days, was quite valuable. Two years later he had his choice between waiting for his money or taking his salary in "weanter fish." Like a wise man he took the fish, holding that a bird in the hand was worth two in the bush.

By degrees, owing to their attachment to strong drink, the people lost the high character which they so long bore. When the Revolutionary war broke out, the most of the inhabitants removed to the mainland, for the reason that the place became the rendezvous of British cruisers. From the close of the war to the year 1800, those left here only had occasional preaching by the Rev. Jeremiah Shaw. In 1790, so indifferent was the tone of feeling, that, as the records say, "Some of the people of the baser sort pulled down and burnt the meeting house." The writer who records the act continues: "The special judgment of heaven seems to have followed this piece of wickedness to those concerned in it, who seem since to have been given up to work all manner of wickedness with greediness."

Eventually the people of Massachusetts built them a meeting house with stone walls, on Star Island, sent them a teacher, besides food and clothing, and in return received from the inhabitants a promise of reformation. The Rev. Jedidiah Morse preached the opening sermon from Ps. 118: 25.

The teacher of "these unfortunate people," as the Portsmouth *Star* called them at the time, was a Mr. Stevens, who was also their spiritual director and the

Justice of the Peace. He died on Star Island in 1804.

Caleb Chase, of Newburyport, came to the isles to teach school in 1819. Speaking of himself in the book of record he says, that " He endeavored to ascertain the ages of the people generally, but many of them had lost their ages for the want of a record." Also that " When he came to the isles there were on Star Island eleven families and two solitaires, fifty-two souls. On Smutty-nose five families and one solitary, twenty-six souls, and on Hog Island one family, eight souls; in all, eighty-six souls."

The Rev. Samuel Sewell arrived on a " mission," in September, 1824, and found fourteen families and one "solitary" on Star Island, in all sixty-nine persons. In 1832 the population had increased to ninety-nine. From 1804 to 1845 no town meeting was held. Since that period the improvement has been steady, and all the social, political and religious interest cultivated on the mainland are attended to here.

But while I have digressed in giving this historical sketch, the result of much labor, my friends have been kept waiting at the landing, where there is no wharf, but a long inclined plane built of plank, descending under the water, and accommodating itself to every state of the tide. Close by are the boat-houses, and farther on, to the left, is the private residence of the Leighton Brothers. Across the lawn stands the hotel, an enormous building that has twice duplicated its capacity, and now, surmounted by its huge observatory, appears in the distance like some old baronial castle full of quadrangular nooks. We perceive at a glance that there are no more trees on the island than there were in 1624, when Levett landed, yet there is a broad, generous piazza, nearly three hundred feet long, having at the end a high platform large enough for a ball-room, completely roofed in, but open at three sides, and commanding a view of the ocean, both north and south. We hardly miss the trees, as the air is so cool, even rivaling in this respect the atmosphere of Homer's Atlantis. In leaving the mainland there is a complete change, and a fortnight spent here will afford the benefits of an ocean voyage, wholly separated from its often disagreeable experience. In winter also the climate is superior to that of the mainland. Mr. Tucke used to say that in this season the isles were "a thin underwaistcoat warmer" than in the corresponding latitude ashore.

From a careful examination of Appledore, it appears as if the sea once separated it into two islands. A valley terminating in coves at each end runs across it. The southern part is the highest, standing as it does ninety feet above the level of the sea. The northern half accommodates the hotel, which is in the little valley somewhat sheltered from the easterly winter gales.

Ascending to the lofty observatory, which affords a splendid outlook, the uneven, rumpled character of this and the neighboring isles becomes apparent. Since the rocks rose from the bosom of the sea, there have been many convulsions, and earthquakes have opened broad seams which were filled by the molten trap boiling up like lava from below. There is a great deal of interest here, and it is to be regretted that the State Geologists made such a farce of their survey. It appears that they came out to the isles in the revenue cutter one windy day, landed at two or three points, concluded that there was considerable surf running, and then went home again, taking along with them a couple of those barbarous sketches which disfigure so many official reports. In these sketches Gosport and White Island would find it impossible to recognize themselves.

Appledore is just half a nautical mile long and about three-eighths of a mile wide in its broadest or southern part. The walk around it, however it may seem, scarcely exceeds a mile and a half. It is quite fatiguing, but it repays the labor. Here there are none of those tremendous cliffs which at Mount Desert look down upon the sea, and therefore the bold rocky shore may be always followed. In part there is very hard scrambling, by reason of the broad rifts in the granite and gneiss of which the island is composed. The most of these are still paved with dark trap-rock that was originally level with the surface. The peculiar structure of this rock causes it to yield easily to the force of the waves, and thus long galleries are formed in the granite from a distance appearing like the work of man. In sailing around the isles this feature is very noticeable, as the galleries run in some distance at right angles with the beach.

We began our tour at the north side. On our way thither we passed the monument of the late proprietor whose grave is near by. This is a plain memorial fixed firmly in the rock.

Mr. Laighton was a somewhat peculiar character. At one time he took part in New Hampshire politics. He afterwards became dissatisfied with the main, and took charge of White Island Light, where he lived for six years. When attention began to be turned to the isles, he built a small hotel on Appledore for the accommodation of visitors. This hotel has kept pace in its growth with the fame of the isles, which has spread all over the Union. For the last twenty-five years of his life Mr. Laighton never once visited the busy world over the waves. Here he dwelt by himself, occupying the position of Lord of the Isles, and when he died his remains fitly found a resting-place within the sound of the sea which he loved so well.

Arriving at the cove we noticed a couple of fishermen catching perch, using rods, as for trout, notwithstanding the waves were rolling in, booming and blanching, as Tennyson has it, on the rocks.

Turning westward, we came to what is called the Greek Cross, formed by two immense channels in the rock intersecting at right angles. One was formerly filled with a poor metamorphic slate, and the other with trap. Both have been eaten out by the sea. The evidence of volcanic action is here very visible. Long after their original formation, the isles were time after time rent in twain. It may be difficult to realize the fact, yet the time has been when the waves of liquid fire, bursting up from the great molten sea below, vied in their wrath with the ocean wave, while the brine-washed rock hissed at the fiery spray. And will this occur again? Whittier tells us that when

> " Goody Cole looked out from her door,
> The Isles of Shoals were drowned and gone."

This may some day take place in earnest; for we do not know whether the earthquake shocks that have been felt on an average once in ten years at a single spot on yonder main ever since the country was settled, are the dying growls of a tempest that is past, or the mutterings of a storm to come. At any rate let not the proprietors suppose that I am in league with those speculators who would fain buy this isle.

Clambering along among the rocks, we found a broad gulch that might be used as a dry dock. From this point may be had a view of Duck Island with a single old building on it, and lying north-east, distant exactly three-fourths of a nautical mile. Northward, in Maine, is Agamenticus. Westward is Hampton Beach, and Po Hill, which hides Whittier's home. Close to the shore the ledges are everywhere very fine. We returned by the shingle beach on the south shore, having made the circuit of half the island.

It was some time before sunset that we set out to explore the remaining and more interesting portion of Appledore, which is separated from the rest by a stone wall. Passing through a gate, we came upon a flock of sheep, who stared at us for a minute, and then, following their leader, ran. Taking the west side of the island, we walked among the sheep-paths until we reached the ruins of the old settlement. Nothing is left but cellar walls, and the whole vicinage is covered with elderberry bushes, upon which was fruit enough to make hogsheads of wine. Occasionally the ground had a dark rich hue, and here and there something was still left to indicate that " once a garden smiled." The single unoccupied house is of a modern origin, and, standing and uncared for and alone, it looks as if haunted.

The reason why this spot was so soon deserted is clear. The fishermen had no beach for their boats. The only place to land was in a chasm about twenty-five feet wide with perpendicular walls, formed by the disintegration of the trap-rock. This was of course insufficient, and accordingly they sought the shelter of Star and Haley.

Farther eastward another earthquake record is found in what has been called Neptune's Gallery, with perpendicular scarred walls, high and far apart, between which the breakers roll in with a sound that is well nigh deafening. Near this point the rocks are high and bold. Farther on, around the point, a cove makes into the shore, the rocks being ragged and disjointed, and piled up in the greatest confusion. Returning thence, we crossed the centre of the island and approached the cairn, which we had understood was Smith's Monument, lately erected to his memory. This cairn is about ten feet high, bulging at one side, and seeming to incline like "Pisa's leaning miracle." Determined to do the great adventurer homage, I shouldered a good-sized fragment of granite, and staggered towards the cairn, while Amarinta followed by my side, bearing a tribute of more delicate proportions. These were reverently added to the pile; and, *mens conscia recti*, that is to say, happy in the delusion of a duty well done, we sat down by the cairn and spoke of the great man's worth. While here the day came to an end, the western clouds, "ministering with glorious faces to the setting sun." At the same time full-orbed Luna appeared in the east, blushing as from our praise of her loveliness. This meeting of Day and Night was as if Righteousness and Peace had kissed each other.

Gradually the splendor of sunset died away, and the dark blue sky at the west shading off at the horizon into deep purple, which threw the inky tones of sepia upon the waves; while eastward, recovering from the embarrassment that attended her first appearance, the moon looked calmly across the silvery track formed by her own bright beams in the shimmering sea. When the moon rose higher, sending lances of light down the western slope of the island into the cove and out across towards the main, the scene changed again, and where before all was indistinguishable in the twilight's gloom, the boats and yachts came out with a fairy-like aspect, rocking on the tide, while the voices of excursionists bound for a moonlight sail were borne to us on the evening air.

On returning to the Appledore House we were quite shocked to learn that our respect for Captain John Smith had been quite thrown away. In fact it appeared that this was not the monument which had been erected to his memory, but one that, according to tradition, was *built* by him. I was quite confused at first on discovering my mistake, but I soon rallied and repaid my informant tenfold, by letting him know, as already stated, that nothing exists to indicate that Smith ever stepped upon these isles. I cruelly followed this up the next day by ferreting out unimpeachable testimony which proves that the cairn was erected only about seventy years ago as a mark for fishermen in finding the bearing of their fishing grounds.

Boating at the Isles of Shoals is a favorite amusement. One pleasant day we rowed to a number of different points. Our first harbor was Londonner's or Lounging Island, a rocky spot three-fourths of a nautical mile south-west from the cove at Appledore. The north and south halves of this island, which is three-sixteenths of a mile long, are connected by a narrow neck often covered at high tide, the mean rise and fall of which is eight feet six inches. Entering the cove on the east side, we found the Hibernian fisherman, who dwells here, out in a boat catching perch with which to bait his trawls for cod. He told what he knew about his craft, after which we put into one of those convenient docks formed by the erosion of trap dykes, and went ashore. The Hibernian in question *can* say with Caliban, "This island's mine." He seemed a sort of Caliban himself, and his boys young Calibans. A battered wooden cottage takes the place of a cave, but I found no enchanter. It appears to have had as hard usage as its owner. A fish-like odor pervaded the air, a goat was paying attention to the moss on the rocks, while some chickens and ducks were picking up a living around the door. We looked into the fish-house, and hurried away, quite satisfied with what we saw.

Three-fourths of a mile eastward is the head of White Island. This island is nearly one-fourth of a mile long, and about one-sixteenth of a mile wide. Here stands the light-house. From this point Portsmouth Light bears nearly north north-west; Boon Island, distant nineteen and a half miles, bears north-east by north, three-fourths east; and Rye Meeting-house, nine miles distant, north-west by west, one-half west. The Head is separated from the rest of the island at high tide.

Towards this spot we now turned the prow, escorted by a lad who volunteered to serve as pilot. When we approached the landing at the light-house, he told us that he had never been ashore, and he now thought there was too much surf. He accordingly backed his boat off, and we rowed in to reconnoitre. While considering the subject, the Light Keeper, who was on the main rock, seeing our situation, came down to the little bar where the surf was breaking, and, watching his chance, ran through the water and came opposite to us. Then when a convenient wave rolled in, we rushed the boat head on to the beach, the keeper running in to catch her bows. Our venture was successful, but before the windlass could be put in motion to haul the boat up the ways, a second wave, to the great consternation of Amarinta, swashed in over the stern a full barrel of brine, causing a precipitate retreat over the thwarts to the bows. Finally the windlass, planted high up the beach, was at work, and the boat was drawn up out of the surf. The keeper then led the way to the top of the light-house, situated on the highest point of the rock, and reached by a covered bridge. This is a Fresnell light. Its peculiarity is that it has a single burner inclosed in a sort of crystal palace, formed of heavy glass blinds, through which the light passes. At a distance this light shows a great power, though when viewed close at hand, it attracts but little attention. The entire arrangement was imported from France. The first-class lenses cost about ten thousand dollars. Fresnell, the inventor, has now revolutionized the whole light-house system, and conferred a vast benefit upon mankind. This is a flash light, made to give out alternate flashes of red and white, at fifteen seconds each. This lantern has one curious effect. Standing by its side, eighty-seven feet above the water, in a pleasant day it will be found that it gathers up in its mighty focal grasp the objects on Star Island, and sets them down again out at sea. There, for instance, is the meeting-house which stands upon Star Island, planted firmly on the uneasy waves, just as far out in the opposite direction.

The keeper lives here alone with his assistant, maintaining bachelors' hall. In the summer they have a good many visitors, but at other times it is quiet enough; at least, so they say.

And while here I was reminded of a poem that appeared in the *Atlantic* from the pen of Mrs. Thaxter, whose father had charge of the light. It alludes to the wreck of the Brig Pochahontas, lost on the neighboring shore.

Some persons might suppose that this barren rock would prove the last place in which to woo the Muses, yet in all such localities hopeful and receptive minds are not slow in discovering both benefits and beauties. Alexander Smith, wandering for a summer in the rocky island of Skye, almost imagined himself in

Paradise. This is in accordance with the remark of Goethe: "Let no one say that the reality lacks poetical interest." It is both the custom and the right of a class of minds to see everywhere what they please; for there are really no asymptotes in nature. Extremes always meet, barrenness itself running into beauty. It demands no strain upon the imagination in order to discover rare attractions among these isles, especially in the autumn, when the brightest coloring is found, and when from a distance they flash in the blue sea like some huge crystal of iridescent Labrador spar. But we were speaking of the poem. Its merit alone would certainly justify its appearance here, while, as the production of what we may call a resident, its insertion is on the whole demanded:

> "I lit the lamps in the lighthouse tower,
>   For the sun dropped down and the day was dead;
> They shone like a glorious clustered flower,
>   Ten golden and five red.
>
> Looking across, where the line of coast
>   Stretched darkly, shrinking away from the sea,
> The lights sprang out at its edge,—almost
>   They seemed to answer me.
>
> O warning lights, burn bright and clear,
>   Hither the storm comes! Leagues away
> It moans and thunders low and drear,—
>   Burn till the break of day!
>
> Good night! I called to the gulls that sailed
>   Slow past me through the evening sky;
> And my comrades, answering shrilly, hailed
>   Me back with boding cry.

The Isles of Shoals.

A mournful breeze began to blow,
  Weird music it drew through the iron bars,
The sullen billows boiled below,
  And dimly peered the stars;

The sails that flecked the ocean floor
  From east to west leaned low and fled;
They knew what came in the distant roar
  That filled the air with dread!

Flung by a fitful gust, there beat
  Against the window a dash of rain:
Steady as tramp of marching feet
  Strode on the hurricane.

It smote the waves for a moment still,
  Level and deadly white for fear;
The bare rock shuddered,—an awful thrill
  Shook even my tower of cheer.

Like all the demons loosed at last,
  Whistling and shrieking, wild and wide,
The mad wind raged, and strong and fast
  Rolled in the rising tide.

And soon in ponderous showers the spray,
  Struck from the granite, reared and sprung,
And clutched at tower and cottage gray,
  Where overwhelmed they clung

Half drowning, to the naked rock;
  But still burned on the faithful light,
Nor faltered at the tempest's shock,
  Through all the fearful night.

Was it in vain? That know not we.
  We seemed, in that confusion vast
Of rushing wind and roaring sea,
  One point whereon was cast

The whole Atlantic's weight of brine.
  Heaven help the ship should drift our way!
No matter how the light might shine
  Far on into the day.

When morning dawned above the din
   Of gale and breaker boomed a gun!
Another! We, who sat within,
   Answered with cries each one.

Into each other's eyes with fear
   We looked, through helpless tears, as still,
One after one, near and more near,
   The signals pealed, until

The thick storm seemed to break apart,
   To show us, staggering to her grave,
The fated brig. We had no heart
   To look, for naught could save.

One glimpse of black hull heaving slow,
   Then closed the mists o'er canvas torn
And tangled ropes, swept to and fro
   From masts that raked forlorn.

Weeks after, yet ringed round with spray,
   Our island lay, and none might land;
Though blue the waters of the bay
   Stretched calm on either hand.

And when at last from the distant shore
   A little boat stole out, to reach
Our loneliness, and bring once more
   Fresh human thought and speech,

We told our tale, and the boatmen cried:
   ''Twas the Pocahontas,—all were lost!
For miles along the coast the tide
   Her shattered timbers tost.'

Then I looked the whole horizon round,—
   So beautiful the ocean spread
About us, o'er those sailors drowned!
   'Father in heaven,' I said,

A child's grief struggling in my breast,
   'Do purposely thy creatures meet
Such bitter death? How was it best
   These hearts should cease to beat?

'O wherefore! Are we naught to thee?
  Like senseless weeds that rise and fall
Upon thine awful sea, are we
  No more then, after all?'

And I shut the beauty from my sight,
  For I thought of the dead that lay below,
From the bright air faded the warmth and light,
  There came a chill like snow.

Then I heard the far-off rote resound,
  Where the breakers slow and slumberous rolled,
And a subtle sense of Thought profound
  Touched me with power untold.

And like a voice eternal spake,
  That wondrous rhythm, and 'Peace, be still!'
It murmured; 'bow thy head, and take
  Life's rapture and life's ill,

And wait. At last all shall be clear.'
  The long, low, mellow music rose
And fell, and soothed my dreaming ear
  With infinite repose.

Sighing, I climbed the lighthouse stair,
  Half forgetting my grief and pain;
And while the day died, sweet and fair,
  I lit the lamps again."

On leaving the island we had to watch our chance, notwithstanding it was such pleasant weather. First the Assistant got off in a little boat to pick us up in case of a mishap. This was very easily done, as he was used to it, and then we ran our boat down and put Amarinta in, protesting, and declaring that it would *never* do. The right minute came, we shoved out on the undertow, sprang to the oars, and were safe. Getting off at a convenient distance, we find that the head on which the lighthouse stands is a very beautiful object, and, with a fishing-smack thrown in, would, make a fine picture.

Our course was next shaped for Star Island or Gosport, the western cove of which is thirteen-sixteenths of a mile from the lighthouse. There is no wharf and never has been here, though in 1766 the people petitioned for the privilege of getting up a lottery to build one. At low water it is difficult to get ashore, but there is no trouble generally on account of the surf. By making a bridge of skiffs we reached the sandy beach with dry shoes.

Gosport is five-eighths of a mile long and one half a mile wide, presenting the most perfect picture of a fisherman's village that I have seen on the New-England coast. Reaching the shore, we of course came in contact with the fish, and experienced the "pungent odor of o'erboiling tar," so that, with old Ben Jenson, one would fain "sacrifice two-pence worth of juniper" to appease his offended nose. The children were in force, there being a due proportion of girls and boys, and among the latter, perhaps, some little Enoch Arden. Here they played

> "Among the waste and lumber of the shore,
> Hard coils of cordage, swarthy fishing-nets,
> Anchors of rusty fluke, and boats updrawn;
> And built their castles of dissolving sand."

We made our way through all this customary *debris*, to which was now added the charred remains of a recent fire that destroyed a number of buildings, and reached the narrow way that answered for a street, in which "twa wheelbarrows tremble when they meet." Thence we fared forth, like Æneas at Carthage, to explore the stranger clime, and find what land this might be, and by what inhabitants possessed. To accomplish this the more intelligently, we repaired at once to the house of the worthy and obliging Town Clerk, who brought out the records and put us in immediate connection with both the present and the past, adding various comments at the same time on men and things. Much of what has already been given of the history of Gosport was drawn from this valuable repository, which brainless visitors of these latter days have sought to render still more precious, by entrusting to its keeping their autographs, with remarks.

Having taken numerous notes, we threaded our way to the old meeting-house, concerning which the records have considerable to say. We found the minister there, with his coat off, trowel in hand, and hard at work making repairs. We bade him good morrow, and made bold to say that we hoped he was not daubing with "untempered mortar;" which he trowed not, as it was Roman *cement*. Thus easily we made one another's acquaintance, after which he swung open the door and invited us to enter, showing at the same time the new floor which he had laid down, the seats he had refitted, and the neat chairs that he had made for the pulpit, all of which showed that, like the great Paul, he could labor with his own hands. This good and worthy man came here originally for the benefit of his health, and has since remained for the most of the time, serving the islanders, not only as their minister, but as physician, general adviser and friend. The structure is a quaint one. The tip of the spire is forty-two feet from the ground, and may be seen at a distance of twenty-five miles. The building is richly in keeping with everything on the island. Its little bell hanging in the belfry calls the children to school and the people to church, though the school is now held in a separate building. The weathercock is also worth noticing. When put up, an entry was made in the records, noting that the people found it expensive, and adding the pious, and slightly poetical, remark: "May their own hearts yield to the breathings of the Divine Spirit as that vane does to the winds."

Leaving this venerable place we went southward and found a little burial-ground in a depression of the rocks. It had been prepared with much labor and pious care. The earth had evidently been collected with difficulty, as is the case almost everywhere on the isles. Yet there appears to be no disposition to hew out sepulchres in the rocks. Perhaps they approve the sentiment of that prelate who said with his last breath, "Bury me in the sunshine;" still many of the fishermen never need a tomb, as they suffer hydriotaphia in the sea.

We next turned toward the monument to Captain John Smith. This time we felt sure of our ground, though what made us so positive was not the inscription, which in the glaring light we could hardly decipher, but it was argued from the three heads tipping the corners of the capital of a triangular marble column that rested on a pedestal of gneiss; for did not Captain John Smith relieve three Turks of their cranial appendages on one occasion in single combat? At least he *supposed* that he did, and to commemorate the event named three islands off Cape Ann the Three Turks' Heads. The name did not stick, but his admirers have come to the rescue, and tricked out the story in solid marble. It is to be hoped that the story of that adventure is not quite so apocryphal as his " discovery" of these isles. Still, since the iconoclast has robbed us of the romantic story of Pocahontas, we must receive it with care.

From the general appearance of this monument, we might imagine that a committee of the subjects of the *Sublime Porte* had conspired to make our hero ridiculous, out of revenge for the slaughter inflicted upon their ancestors; yet instead of being the work of three vindictive Turks, it appears to have originated from an equal number of respectable Christians. To save the visitor from the purgatorial task of deciphering the inscriptions, I will put them into legible print. On one side we read:

" John Smith was born at Willoughby, Linconshire,

England, in 1579, and died in London in 1631, aged 52 years. He was Governor of Virginia, and subsequently Admiral of New England. These Isles [im?] properly called Smith's Isles, were discovered by him in April. 1614, while with eight others, in an open boat, he was exploring the coast from Penobscot to Cape Cod."

On another we are told that,

"Capt. John Smith was one of 'nature's noblemen.' In his generosity toward the public he almost forgot himself; those who knew him best loved him most, and say of him : 'In all his proceedings he made virtue his first guide, and experience his second; despising baseness, sloth, pride, and indignity, more than any dangers; he would never allow more for himself than for his soldiers, and to no danger would he expose them which he would not share himself. He would never see any in want of what he had, or could get for them ; he would rather want than borrow, or starve than not pay ; he loved action more than words, and hated covetousness and falsehood more than death ; his adventures were for their lives, and his loss was their deaths.'"

The third face testifies,

" In reward of his valor, the Prince of Transylvania presented to Captain John Smith his picture set in gold, gave him a pension of 300 ducats, and granted him a coat-of-arms bearing three Turks' heads in a shield with the motto : 'Vincere est vivere.' In 1627,

Smith says: 'I have spent five years and more than 500 pounds in the service of Virginia and New England, but in neither have I one foot of land, nor the very house I built with my own hands, and am compelled to see those countries shared before me among those who knew them only by my descriptions.' Consideration of the interesting facts of his life has led to the erection of this monument, A. D. 1864."

Such is the monument that the New World gives to the heroic and magnanimous Captain John Smith. This is the unkindest cut of all. Better far would have been a simple cairn. As one of the explorers of New England, he did good service, although anticipated by Champlain, who has the *prior* right to a monument. His career, when stripped of all fiction, still presents sufficient to admire, and in whatever aspect he may be viewed he will always appear as a remarkable man. He deserved something better than this; built, too, upon the mainland, where his discoveries lay, and upon which he unquestionably trod. But he can afford to wait.

Beyond this place is found what is called Miss Underwood's Rock, named after the teacher of the school, who while sitting here reading a book was swept off by a wave. No less than three young girls have since perished at the same place. Every one who comes here wishes to know how it occurred. Let them in future restrain their curiosity and keep away from the booming surf.

Some distance to the eastward is a huge rift called "Betty Moody's Cave." It is said that in the French war, when the Indians were committing depredations all along the coast, one Betty Moody here secreted herself and children from the wrath of the savages. I give it, however, as a tradition, unsupported by contemporaneous authorities.

Another story is also told in regard to a minister of the same name, who preached to the islanders. It appears that one of their fishing boats had been lost with the entire crew, in Ipswich Bay. During a sermon, in which Mr. Moody sought to "improve" upon this sad event, he said: "Supposing, my brethren, any of you should be overtaken in the bay by a north-east storm, your hearts trembling with fear, and nothing before you but death, whither would your thoughts turn? what would you do?" To this he received the unexpected reply from an old sailor, who, unable to repress himself, promptly said: "I would hoist the foresail and scud away for Squam!"

In this vicinity the rocks are fine and the shore bold, its outline forming the letter M with its top to the islands, not a foot of land now intervening between us and the Old World; yet we did not delay, but returned through the village and went to the north-west end of the island to view the remains of an old fort. On the way, we passed another burial ground, from which it appears that here the living are less numerous than the dead. It is generally the

The Isles of Shoals. 213

case with islands; however fruitful in material products, they consume more than they yield; and if prolific as cradles, they are more bountiful as graves. But let us not meditate among the tombs.

The fort alluded to was in condition prior to the Revolution, and mounted nine four-pounders. When the war broke out they were removed to the main land. The work was constructed chiefly of stone, and could not have had very high walls. It was about fifty feet square. Here is where the Cross of King George floated in colonial times, when the people paid all due respect to the reigning power. One of the last entries in the record book, prior to the dispersion of the people, is dated March 11, 1775. I give it verbatim: "For histing the flag to Henry Andres, 20s." This was probably the final wages of loyalty, for in a few weeks New England was fairly rocked by revolution.

We went thence toward the landing again, passing on the way a fish-house that had been decorated with evergreen from the mainland, preparatory to holding a fair for the benefit of the school. The profusion of young forest trees, with which the place was decorated, led us to think that Birnam's wood had come to Dunsinane. Afterwards we rambled among the houses, and noticed a hotel in process of erection to take the place of an old one destroyed by fire. At the same time we suddenly heard a great shouting on the beach, which was taken up elsewhere, until all

Gosport rang with a hue and a cry, ending with a general rush of old and young for the boats. At first we thought that the island was going down, or at least that a school of porpoises had entered the cove; but ultimately it appeared that the uproar was caused by the arrival of a steamer from Newburyport, loaded with excursionists. In the ears of the Shoalites, the music of the brass band was of itself inspiring, but then what was all this compared with the five hundred dimes prospectively placed in their empty pockets? In their financial economy, it was as reviving as rain upon the parched earth. Accordingly every boy who could paddle a tub, put off from shore, the Town Clerk among the rest, with his yawl, the fleet of boats appearing around the great steamer, like so many minnows around a whale. Soon the whole party was safely put ashore, and went trooping among the rocks to find Betty Moody's Cave, and inaugurate a great day in Gosport.

As for ourselves, we quietly rowed to Haley's Island, or Smutty-Nose, distant one-fourth of a mile. Approaching the landing, we noticed a large brown house with the word "HOTELL" painted in huge letters on one end. At the landing is a wharf, on the east side of which there is room for a couple of vessels that are protected on the east side by a stone wall, which also connects a detached portion of the isle with Smutty Nose. In this inclosed situation a vessel is safe in the heaviest gale. This was built by the person after whom the island was formerly called. How it obtained its present name I could not learn. The " Hotell " did not wear a very inviting appearance, and we passed by and went on a stroll over the island, where we found considerable grass land. In an unenclosed space was the grave of the builder of the dock. A plain stone bore the following rude inscription :

" In memory of Mr. Saml. Haley, who died Feby 7th. 1811 Aged 84. He was a man of great ingenuity, Industry, Honor & honesty, true to his country & A man who did A great publik good in Building A Dock & Receiving into his inclosure many a poor distressed Seaman & Fisherman in distress of Weather."

Near by may also be seen the Spaniards' Graves, where lie the remains of fourteen shipwrecked sailors, each marked by a rude stone. It is to their fate that Whittier refers when he brings forward his old fisherman, lean as a cusk from Labrador, who told of wrecks and storms, had seen the sea-serpent,

> "And heard the ghosts on Haley's Isle complain,
> Speak him off shore, and beg a passage to old Spain."

Of the islanders, nothing definite could be learned about this affair; but, in searching the records of Gosport, I found the following entry :

" Ship Sagunto Strand^{ed} on Smotinose Ile Jan^{y}14— 1813. Jany 15 one man foun 16th 6 mend found 21— 7 the Number of men yet found Belonging to said ship twelve." The scribe dropped two in his addition.

From some old newspapers of the day, it appears that this ship was from Cadiz, loaded with provisions, and commanded by a Captain Don. She went to pieces soon after stranding, and a portion of the cargo, consisting of nuts and raisins, was thrown upon the shore, together with bales of clothing made of broadcloth. It was also believed that the ship contained considerable money, as gold and silver coins were washed out upon the shore. The ship was of three or four hundred tons capacity, built of cedar and mahogany, and very old. One account says that, "Much credit is due to the inhabitants of these barren rocks for their instantaneous launching forth their boats in a violent snow storm, the moment they discovered the wreck, in hope of being able to rescue from a watery grave the crew of the ship." Mrs. Thaxter writes :

> " O sailors, did sweet eyes look after you,
>   The day you sailed away from sunny Spain ?
> Bright eyes that followed fading ship and crew,
>   Melting in tender rain ?
>
> Did no one dream of that drear night to be,
>   Wild with the wind, fierce with the stinging snow,
> When, on yon granite point that frets the sea,
>   The ship met her death-blow ?
>
> Fifty long years ago these sailors died :
>   (None know how many sleep beneath the waves:)
> Fourteen gray headstones, rising side by side,
>   Point out their nameless graves,—

> Lonely, unknown, deserted, but for me,
>   And the wild birds that flit with mournful cry,
>   And sadder winds, and voices of the sea
>   That moans perpetually.
>
> Wives, mothers, maidens, wistfully, in vain
>   Questioned the distance for the yearning sail,
> That, leaning landward, should have stretched again
>   White arms wide on the gale,
>
> To bring back their beloved. Year by year,
>   Weary they watched, till youth and beauty passed,
> And lustrous eyes grew dim, and age drew near,
>   And hope was dead at last.
>
> Still summer broods o'er that delicious land,
>   Rich, fragrant, warm with skies of golden glow:
> Live any yet of that forsaken band
>   Who loved so long ago?
>
> O Spanish women, over the far seas,
>   Could I but show you where your dead repose!
> Could I send tidings on this northern breeze,
>   That strong and steady blows!
>
> Dear dark-eyed sisters, you remember yet
>   These you have lost, but you can never know
> One stands at their bleak graves whose eyes are wet
>   With thinking of your woe!"

This island is half a mile long and less in width. The land is flat. On the western part there is considerable good grass. A woman by the name of Pusley died here in 1795. She kept two cows somewhere on one of the isles, and cut in the summer all the hay they needed in winter with a knife. The poor woman's cows were taken by the British in 1775 and killed. To their credit we must add that they paid for them. It is related, however, that she was inconsolable. The cattle and sheep do very well here now.

There are only a few buildings on the island, though once they boasted of an academy; and it is said, though I cannot verify the report, that at an early period students came here from the mainland to pursue their studies. Possibly they came as well to save their scalps as to improve the region situated underneath.

And speaking of houses reminds me of another story, to the effect that a storm once carried away one of the houses entire to Cape Cod, where it was tossed up on *terra firma*. They learned where it came from by some papers preserved in a box. It is an excellent story, at least.

This is a pleasant, sunny island where rambling will be found pleasant, even though the historical associations are of less interest than at Gosport.

As we returned to Appledore the yacht *Celia* was just leaving for Portsmouth, and the Brothers Laighton were giving a parting salute with the bell and horn, the latter an instrument about three feet long, which can at least boast of some power. We pitied from the bottom of our hearts the poor wights who were now returning to the world; but soon got over our concern for them and "sadly thought of the morrow"— the morrow, fated day—when we, too, must bid farewell to these sunny isles and in turn become the objects of commisseration.

Thus the bright days pass at the Isles of Shoals. After the round has thus been gone through, it then remains to be gone through again with variations, each time meeting some new view or odd adventure. For those fond of studying marine flora, there are unbounded facilities. At low water, in a sunny day, drift in your boat along past the northwest point of Star Island, at the right distance from the rocks, and observe, far down, the beautiful groves of waving fronds that fill this watery world, with the perch as tame as kittens, feeding upon salads of bright green sea-lettuce. By dredging we shall find that each successive depth has its peculiarities. There are zones on the mountains under the water, along those dim slopes that descend to the ocean's lowest depths, as well as on the heights above. If we could descend, what marvels should we behold! There the carnival of color is perpetual, running riotously through the whole chromatic scale, while the deep-sea fruits are ever ripening on their graceful stems. We have an earnest of what we might expect, both in the gorgeous coloring of the mosses that the waves toss upon the beach, and in the "salt lemons and oranges that come up on the dredge."

The flora upon the land is also more promising than it may appear at first sight. It is tolerably well catalogued in another poem by Mrs. Thaxter, entitled "Rockweeds."

"So bleak these shores, wind-swept, and all the year
  Washed by the wild Atlantic's restless tide,
You would not dream that flowers the woods hold dear
  Amid such desolation dare abide.

Yet when the bitter winter breaks, some day,
  With soft winds fluttering her garments' hem,
Up from the sweet South comes the lingering May,
  Sets the first wind-flower trembling on its stem.

Scatters her violets with lavish hands,
  White, blue, and amber; calls the columbine
Till, like clear flame in lonely nooks, gay bands
  Swinging their scarlet bells obey the sign;

Makes buttercups and dandelions blaze,
  And throws in glimmering patches here and there
The little eyebright's pearls, and gently lays
  The impress of her beauty everywhere.

Later, June bids the sweet wild-rose to blow,
  Wakes from its dream the drowsy pimpernel;
Unfolds the bindweed's ivory buds, that glow
  As delicately blushing as a shell.

Then purple Iris smiles; and hour by hour
  The fair procession multiplies; and soon
In clusters creamy white, the elder flower
  Waves its broad disk against the rising moon.

O'er quiet beaches shelving to the sea
  Tall mulleins sway, and thistles: all day long
Comes in the wooing water dreamily,
  With subtle music in its slumbrous song.

Herb-Robert hears, and princess-feather bright,
  While goldthread clasps the little skull-cap blue;
And troops of swallows, gathering for their flight,
  O'er golden rod and asters hold review.

The Isles of Shoals.

The barren island dreams in flowers, while blow
    The south winds, drawing haze o'er sea and land;
Yet the great heart of ocean, throbbing slow,
    Makes the frail blossoms visible where they stand.

And hints of heavier pulses soon to shake
    Its mighty breast when summer is no more,
When devastating waves swoop on and break,
    And clasp with girdle white the iron shore.

Close-folded, safe within the sheltering seed,
    Blossom and bell and leafy beauty hide;
Nor icy blast nor bitter spray they heed,
    But patiently their wondrous change abide.

The heart of God through his creation stirs;
    We thrill to feel it, trembling as the flowers
That die to live again,—his messengers
    To keep faith firm in these sad souls of ours.

The waves of Time may devastate our lives,
    The frosts of age may check our failing breath;
They shall not touch the spirit that survives
    Triumphant over doubt and pain and death."

PENOBSCOT BAY.

CHAPTER XIV.

KENNEBEC — MONHEGAN — CAMDEN — OLDTOWN — PAMOLA — CASTINE — THE CAPUCHINS — ISLE OF HAUTE — PLACENTIA — MOUNT DESERT.

ENOBSCOT Bay lies in a region invested with all the interest that is attached to other portions of the Maine Coast. In going thither from the Isles of Shoals, we pass outside of Casco Bay, which, with its countless islands and numerous delightful resorts, might well claim a chapter of its own. But making Portland the point of departure, we go *through* this bay, and, if it is daylight, become somewhat acquainted with its peculiarities. After clearing the bay in the night, the first light that appears is Seguin. This stands near the mouth of that beautiful stream, the Kennebec. When on the coast of Maine, the summer tourist should ascend this river to Augusta. The scenery is everywhere fine. Here for the first time we saw a sturgeon, as described by Longfellow, in all his armor:

> " On each side a shield to guard him,
> Plates of bone upon his forehead,
> Down his sides, back and shoulders,

> Plates of bone with spines projecting!
> Painted was he with his war paint,
> Stripes of yellow, red and azure,
> Spots of brown and spots of sable."

They always seem very fond of leaping out of the water. Standing on the deck of the upward-bound steamer, we heard a sudden splash in the water, and started, thinking that a man had fallen overboard; but it proved to be only "the sturgeon, Nahma," who from the bottom

> " rose with angry gesture,
> Quivering in each nerve and fibre,
> Clashing all his plates of armor,
> Gleaming bright with all his war paint;
> In his wrath he darted upward,
> Flashing leaped into the sunshine."

While I was looking at the place where he disappeared, Nahma's brother, about the size of a man, did precisely the same thing, leaping full out of the water, and then falling back again in true histrionic style, as if stiff and dead.

Next on our right, at sea, is Monhegan. This is a low flat island of considerable size. Beyond question Captain John Smith actually landed here, if he did not at the Isles of Shoals. We have his own word for it. He arrived in April, 1614. The island had been a resort of fishermen since 1608, if not longer. Smith says that "whilst the sailors fished, myself with eight others ranged the coast in a small boat. We got for trifles near eleven thousand beaver skins, one hundred martens, and as many otters." He carried back to England forty-seven thousand dried fish cured at the island. The Arabic system of notation would utterly fail to tell how many thousand cod have been taken here since. The settlement on the island is small, but the place is of genuine interest. We passed this island again on one of the loveliest nights that I ever spent on the water, when the full-orbed moon sent down upon the waves her most bewitching glances. For

> "In such a night
> Stood Dido with a willow in her hand
> Upon the wild sea banks and waft her love
> To come again to Carthage."

If the runaway Æneas had been with us on the Lewiston, he would not have objected seriously to going anywhere, simply on account of the weather.

On this island is what looks like a Runic inscription in the face of a rock. An engraving of this rock is given by the Society of Northern Antiquarians in one of their publications (*Des Antiquaires du Nord*, May 14, 1859), but the Society very prudently abstained from giving an opinion. The Northmen when on the coast may have noticed this island, yet the alleged inscription is probably the result of disintegration.

Opposite Monhegan, on the main, is Pemaquid, the home of Samoset, who welcomed the English Pilgrims at Plymouth in 1620. Bradford says this

Chief came "boulddly amongst them, and spoke to them in broken English, which they could well understand but marvelled at it. At length they understood by discourse with him, that he was not one of these [Plymouth] parts, but belonged to ye eastrene parts, wher some English ships came to fish, with whom he was acquainted, and could name sundrie of them by their names, amongst whom he gott his language." According to the account which he gave of himself, he was Sagamore of "Morattiggon," lying eastward "a daye's sail with a great wind, and five days by land." He visited the Pilgrims again two days afterwards, that is, Sunday, March 18; and on March 22, he came for the last time to Plymouth with the Chief Squanto, by whose joint agency a peace was arranged with Massasoit.

He appears only once more on the page of New England history, in 1625, when he deeded away a large tract of land near Pemaquid. Among his other good acts was that of rescuing some shipwrecked Frenchmen cast away on Cape Cod in 1617. Says one writer, "The life of the Pemaquid chief Samoset, or Somerset, must ever awaken the most tender and interesting reflections; and the generosity and genuine nobility of soul, displayed by this son of the forest, must be allowed as a fairer index to the true character of the Aborigines than their deeds of resentment and cruelty in after-days, when goaded to madness by the cupidity or treachery of the Europeans."

Between Pemaquid and Monhegan the fight of the Enterprise and the Boxer took place in 1813, the latter becoming a prize to the United States, after a severe engagement of thirty-five minutes, in which the commanders were both killed.

Early in the morning the steamer reaches Rockland, where the Portland steamer connects with the boat running to Bangor. This place is chiefly celebrated for its lime, which is burnt and exported in fabulous quantities. Our Down-east friends find the lime-rock as good as gold, and get rich in the trade almost as fast as their Massachusetts neighbors do in selling off their ice. From this point we catch a glimpse of the Camden Hills, a few miles distant, now a popular place of resort. The whole region around Camden abounds in attractions that have not become hackneyed like most of the resorts in Massachusetts. The hills as we passed them strikingly reminded us of the heights of Mount Desert, though they present little of their wonderful variety.

The coast line here as everywhere is extremely irregular. Between Portland and Machiasport the steamer changes her course over two hundred times. From Kittery Point to West Quoddy Head, the distance in a right line is only about two hundred and twenty-six miles, while it is said that an actual survey will make the shore three thousand.

So little was known of the coast in 1607, that Popham wrote to Prince Charles, telling him that nutmegs and cinnamon grew here. He also said that seven days' journey westward from Sagadahoc, there was a large sea reaching to China, which "unquestionably" was not far from these shores.

A short distance above Bangor is the settlement of the Old Town Indians. The present number of the tribe is five hundred and twenty-five. The school numbers fifty-four scholars. They receive from the Government nearly six thousand dollars annually. Their number has not diminished for the last forty years. They are frequently seen in the vicinity of Mount Desert. They have a "New Party," and an "Old Party," as is the case at Pleasant Point, though with the Old Town Indians the New Party is the less respectable. They have had bitter quarrels among themselves from time to time, and once, for a period of two years, they were left by the Roman Catholic authorities, to whose church they adhere, as perfectly incorrigible. They have among them a Phenician custom which prevails in Ireland, of building huge bonfires on Midsummer Eve, the Vigil of S. John Baptist. They are exceedingly superstitious, and have some famous traditions regarding Mount Katahdin, the residence of the Spirit Pamola. One of them, according to Father Vetromile, who served as Priest of Old Town, runs as follows:

Several hundred years ago, while a Penobscot Indian was encamped east of Katahdin, in the autumn hunting season, an unexpected fall of snow covered the whole country to the depth of many feet. Not having any snow-shoes, he was unable to return home, and remained blocked up in the drifts, feeling that he must eventually perish. But in his despair he called with a loud voice for Pamola, who finally made his appearance on the top of the mountain. Thereupon the Indian took courage, and offered a sacrifice of oil and fat, which he poured upon some burning coals. As the smoke went up, Pamola descended from the summit of the mountain, when the sacrifice was repeated, drawing Pamola as far as the camp, where the Indian welcomed him, saying. "You are welcome, Partner." Pamola replied: "You have done well to call me partner, for thus you are saved, who otherwise would have been destroyed by me. Now I will take you on the mountain, and you shall be happy with me." He therefore put the Indian on his shoulders, bade him close his eyes, and in a few minutes, with a noise as of a whistling wind, they were inside of the mountain. The Indian described the interior of Katahdin as containing a comfortable wigwam, furnished with an abundance of venison, and all the luxuries of life, and that Pamola had a wife and children living there. Pamola gave him his daughter to wife, and told him that after one year he could return to his friends at the Penobscot, and have the privilege of coming to see his wife as often as he pleased. He was told, however, that he must not marry another wife, and that if he did he would immediately be transported to Katahdin, from whence he would never return again. At the end of the year he went back to Old Town and told all his adventures. The Indians urged him to marry again, which at first he refused to do; though at last they carried their point. But Pamola was true to his word, for the day after he suddenly disappeared, and he must, of course, have been spirited back to the heart of the Mountain. It is to be hoped that his fate will have a wholesome effect upon those who remain. I was shown by Dr. Ballard, the Secretary of the Maine Historical Society, a rude sketch of Pamola, that was made for him by an Indian. The sketch reminded me of Falstaff's description of Slender, who "was for all the world like a forked radish, with a head fantastically carved on it with a knife."

We did not on this occasion ascend the Penobscot, which, however, well repays the journey, as the steamer sailed from Rockland direct to Castine. This is another extremely interesting place. As we approached the landing, the old earthworks upon the summit of the hill to the rear of the town came prominently into view, their outline being relieved by the sky. Castine has a pleasant, cleanly appearance, and the whole neighborhood looks inviting. Near the Point is shown the site of Baron Castin's fort.

Among the names associated with the early days of the Penobscot that of Vincent de St. Castin is the most distinguished. At one time he was an officer in the body guard of the King of France. Born near the Pyrenees and accustomed to their wild and rugged scenery, the primeval forests of Acadie accorded well with his eccentric disposition. Soon after arriving at Quebec, in 1665, the regiment of which he was commander having been disbanded, he selected the pine-clad peninsula of Bignatus as his place of residence. On the same spot which had previously been occupied by D'Aulney and Temple, he erected a fortified habitation, and for over a quarter of a century carried on an extensive and profitable trade. La Hontan estimated his profits to have been two or three hundred thousand crowns, and Castin himself informed M. Tibierge, in 1695, that eighty thousand livres could be annually realized at Penobscot out of the beaver trade. In 1673, twenty-one white persons, including soldiers, were connected with Castin's establishment. He formed a close alliance with the savages by marrying the daughter of Madackawando, their chief, and his influence over them was so great, that they regarded him as their tutelar god. Within his habitation was a chapel attended by a Roman priest. He was an avowed enemy of the English. King William's War has sometimes been called Castin's War. In 1688 Sir Edmund Andros anchored off his fort in the frigate Rose, when the Baron fled to the woods. Andros landed and pillaged the place, not even respecting the chapel altar. Then followed nine years of war and bloodshed. Castin afterwards rebuilt his fort, but while absent in France in 1703, it was again pillaged. The next year Colonel Church carried fire and the sword throughout the region. Castin died in France, but his son by his Indian wife continued to live in the country.

The visitor at modern Castine may also feel interested in learning that at one period the Capuchins had established a monastery here. This Order is a branch of the Friars Minor, founded by St. Francis of Assissi. A member of this branch of the Order, having made the remarkable discovery that the brethren did not wear the same style of capuce, or hood, that their founder wore, succeeded, in conjunction with another devotee, in obtaining (July 13. 1528) a Papal Bull for the establishment of the Capuchins as a distinct society. Mr. Shea says that they first appeared in the French colony in 1632, when they were offered the direction of religious affairs, which offer was declined. In 1643 D'Aulney invited them to come to Acadia. In 1646 Father Druillettes, a Jesuit from Quebec, going on a visit to the Abenakis, found at Pentegoet a little hospice of Capuchins, under their Superior, Father Ignatius of Paris. This hospice, according to Charlevoix, was on the Kennebec at Castine, where they acted as Chaplains to the French traders and settlers. It is thought that the visit of Father Druillettes led to the erection of a new and more permanent hospice. At all events one was erected in 1648, which is demonstrated by an inscription on a plate of copper, found in the autumn of 1863, near the old brick battery, known as the Lower Fort. The inscription is as follows:

"1648. 8. IVN. F. LEO. PARISIN. CAPUC. MISS POSVI HOC FVNDTM IN HNR EM NRÆ DMÆ SANCTÆ SPEI."

This may be rendered as follows:

"1648. JAN. 8. I, FRIAR LEO, OF PARIS, CAPUCHIN MISSIONARY, LAID THIS FOUNDATION IN HONOR OF OUR LADY OF HOLY HOPE."

In 1649, D'Aulney, the patron of the Capuchins, was overpowered by La Tour, whom Mr. Shea describes as a "hickory member" of the Roman Catholic Church, and his settlements were disbanded. The Capuchins in Maine left no records.

Of the character of these men we cannot speak with the same definiteness as of the Jesuits. The monks of old differed greatly in their characters and reputation. There were the monks of St. Gildas de Rhuys. Longfellow thus makes Lucifer hit them off in "The Golden Legend":

> "The convent windows gleamed as red
> As the fiery eyes of the monks within,
> Who with jovial din
> Gave themselves up to all kinds of sin!
> Ha! that is a convent! that is an abbey!
> Over the doors,
> None of your death-heads carved in wood,
> None of your Saints looking pious and good,
> None of your Patriarchs old and shabby?
> But the heads and tusks of boors,
> And the cells

> Hung all round with the fells
> Of the fallow deer,
> And then what cheer!
> What jolly fat friars,
> Sitting round the great, roaring fires."

But if the monks of Maine belonged to this class, they showed little sense in leaving the endowed monastery of the Old World for the log-built hospice of the New, where, instead of securing the deer's fell, they might lose their own scalps. They led a hard and often a sad life. Instead of the constant carnival of de Rhuys it was a prolonged Lenten fast. Theirs was the coarse fare, the scanty board, the wearing vigil, the painful march, and, at night, the bed of boughs. Such men have a right to stickle about the cut of a capuce. Indeed, they have seldom had justice. Still they were generally men of right aims and a self-denying spirit, ready to compass sea and land to make a proselyte, and buying at any price the privilege of sending an Indian child to heaven with a drop of dew.

From Castine we descend the bay around Cape Rosier to the pleasant little town of Sedgwick where passengers are landed. Thence the steamer's course is shaped for Deer Isle, which is about half as large as Mount Desert and supports a thicky settled fishing community. The isle appears to be a bright sunny place, and a summer spent here would no doubt be profitable, as the steamer regularly places travellers on one of the most central portions of the bay.

We next go through Egemoggin Reach which extends between Deer Isle and the mainland, after which the Isle au Haute, High Island, as Champlain called it. That explorer was evidently well acquainted with this locality. He says: "Coming to the south of the High (*haute*) island, and coasting it at about one-fourth of a league where there are several sand-bars just out of water, we turned to the west till we opened the mountains which are to the north of said island. You can be assured that in seeing the eight or nine notches in the Isle of Mount Desert and of Bedabebec, you will not see any more islands." It was on the Isle of Haute that the United States Sloop-of-War, John Adams, mounting twenty-four guns, got ashore August 17, 1814, having on board sixty English prisoners. She was eventually brought off and taken up the Penobscot, where to prevent her capture by the British, she was set on fire.

Close at hand may also be seen Placentia, an island that Whittier celebrates in his poem of Mogg Megone. He tells us of one Pere Breteaux who had a mission there, dwelling alone in a hut. He says:

> "There sleep Placentia's group—and there
> Pere Breteaux marks the hour of prayer;
> And there, beneath the sea-worn cliff,
>   On which the Father's Hut is seen
> The Indian stays his rocking skiff,
>   And peers the hemlock bough between,
> Half trembling as he seeks to look
> Upon the Jesuits Cross and Book."

This, however, is nothing but a pretty fiction. No mission ever existed here, and no Jesuit of the name ever labored on the Maine Coast. It is, nevertheless, a pleasant spot.

Speaking of Mount Desert, Champlain says that it is close to the main land, "and very high and notched, appearing from the sea like what seems to be seven or eight mountains on a line near each other," which has already been shown to be the case. The summits appeared then as they do now, for he says, " the tops of the most of them are without trees, because all is rocks." What woods there were he says were "all pines and *boilleaus*." He adds, " I named it the Island of the Desert Mountain," (*iles Monts desert.*) The latitude of the highest eminence, Green Mountain, he fixed at forty-four and a half, which agrees sufficiently well with the modern survey.

Then we left Penobscot Bay and sailed around Mount Desert to South-West Harbor, where Colonel Church, during the French and Indian war, sometimes came in search of the enemy, who made the isle a rendezvous. It was here in a cask that the Massachusetts men established a novel post-office. Arriving here Church says that he found none of his vessels that he expected, but instead "a rundlet rid off by a line in the harbor which he ordered to be taken up." On opening it he found a letter addressed to him, from which he learned that the friends had returned to Boston. But on our arrival (1868) we received the mail in a red leather bag, marked *U. S.*, at the hand of Deacon Clark. From thence we steamed around to Bar Harbor, where for the time we bade Captain Deering adieu, intending to start for Grand Menan under his careful and skilful guidance the next trip.

GRAND MENAN.

CHAPTER XV.

ROUTE TO MACHIAS — THE FIGHT — LUBEC — EARLY HISTORY — EXPLORATIONS — GULLS — SWALLOW TAIL HEAD — WHALE COVE — INDIAN BEACH — DARK HARBOR — THE RETURN.

LEAVING Bar Harbor at noon on a beautiful August day, we started for the northern head of Grand Menan, situated in a direct line about eighty-five miles from Mount Desert. In steaming out we had a fine view of the cliffs of Iron-bound Island, and Schoodic Hill. The latter, as we progressed, turned itself around to afford a full view of its bare and bleached sides. Gradually, Newport and Green Mountain faded into one, and then sank out of sight.

The next noticeable feature was Petit Menan, so called to distinguish it from Great, or Grand Menan. It is a low, barren island, with a granite lighthouse one hundred and twenty-five feet high, showing a flash light. A wreck lay in the surf on the beach. This place is about fifteen miles from Bar Harbor. The next lighthouse is on Pond Island, to the right of which is the island called Jordan's Delight, having handsome cliffs. Near a shingle beach was an archway in the rocks. The pilot said that the place was full of attractions.

At Millbridge, it being low water, the passengers were taken off by a boat. Ship's-Stern Island was next pointed out. It resembles, at one end, the stern of an old-fashioned ship. Pigeon Hill now disappeared in the distance, and the steamer ran on among clusters of low, rocky islands, more or less covered with pines, and passed through Plummer's Sound, which forms a fine harbor about six miles long. It is shut in by a range of islands that are famous for shipwrecks.

Next Jonesport, about thirty miles from Bar Harbor, comes in view, with the waters of Moose-A-Beck Reach; Mark Island lying out at the entrance. Jonesport is pleasantly situated. A few houses are scattered near the shore, and further on is a small village. It was from this place that the colonists went forth to settle at Joppa. It does not look like a place capable of producing romantic visionaries like those who undertook to revolutionize Palestine. Opposite lie numerous small islands with a few poor cottages. Jonesport is noted for its fine trout fishing. It has a new hotel, and will erelong become a popular resort. Next the mouth of Englishman's Bay is passed, with Shorey's Island. In the distance, at sea, Pulpit or Split Rock appears, a little to the right of which is the saddle-shaped island known as the Brothers. Next is Green Island, curiously formed, and surmounted by conical-shaped hills. A large flock of gulls was resting on the nearest. Other islands constantly rise up as we pass. Among them is Libbey's Island with its lighthouse, Pettigrew's, Cross Island with its deer and cave containing buried gold which unfortunately no one can find, and Stone's and Brown's Island. On Stone's was a fish-hawks' nest in the top of a dead tree. Passing these, Yellow Head is next seen standing at the west entrance of Machias Bay, with Chauncey's Island on the east. Buck's Harbor is a snug little place near Yellow Head. Numerous other islands are sprinkled about, adding to the beauty of the bay.

Here again we were on historic ground, and were reminded of the celebrated fight off Machias. One of the natives, who knew every inch of land and water in this vicinity, but unfortunately was not posted in history, undertook to tell me how it was.

"You see," said he, "when they found out what the British were about, they just filled the hold of the sloop with men armed with pitchforks and pikes, covered the deck with sheep, and then sailed down the harbor. When they got alongside the British they asked them if they wanted to trade, and when they said they did, the men rushed up out of the hold and took the British in a minute." This was making tolerably short work of it.

From Machias, which bears numerous scars of war, we proceeded twenty-six miles overland to Lubec by

stage. This is the nearest point of departure for
Grand Menan. The road thither is pleasant, and, on
approaching the end, the island lying out against
the horizon presented a long, level, purple wall. Of
Lubec not much can be said. There are some mines
of silver and lead near, and it is not without attractions as a fishing village; yet, on the whole, we concluded that it was a good place to get away from.
This, however, is not such an easy matter, if one's
course lies towards the sea. The steamer which runs
from Boston to Eastport will connect the tourist with
the packet sailing weekly from the latter place to
Grand Menan, usually leaving on Saturday and returning to Eastport the following Wednesday. But
of the packet we could learn nothing. They did not
know whether she had dropped down from Eastport
(three miles above) or not. In fact, while it was
utterly impossible for a tom-cod to pass the docks
night or day without being seen and caught, the good
people knew no more of the packet than some of the
revenue officers here know (perhaps) about smug-
gling. The sum of the whole matter was, that, if I
wished to go to Menan, I had better hire a boat. I
thought so too, on the whole, as the weather was fine
and the breeze fresh and fair. The fishermen with
whom I spoke seemed to think this a happy decision;
and now who should have the job? I finally bar-
gained with a good honest fellow for a five-ton herring boat and a crew of two men. We (that is, Ama-

rinta and I) then hurried on board with our baggage. The skipper brought down a compass, some hard bread, and a jug of water, and at once we were sweeping down the harbor past Campo Bello, favored by wind and tide.

Being now fairly on the way, there was an opportunity to count up the difficulties of the voyage. The distance from West Quoddy Head to Menan is only about nine miles, yet sometimes it takes a week to get across. Fogs, calms, tides and adverse gales combine to stop the passage of a sailing vessel. Pintor, who with his brother artist preceded us, said that they had a hard time of it. Losing the packet, they chartered a fishing boat at Eastport, but got no farther than the east side of Campo Bello, when the fog forced them to take shelter in a fisherman's hut in a cove, for two days and nights. Finally a fishing vessel bound to Menan came into the cove, and, the weather opportunely clearing, they engaged passage and embarked. After beating about the Bay of Fundy all night, they were landed on the east side of Menan in the morning.

For ourselves we happily escaped all this, and so may others, if they carefully lay their plans. Instead of being two days, we made the trip in little more than two hours, as our little craft, under a heavy load of canvas, swept over the wave, like a gull on the wing.

As we advanced, Menan gradually rose above the

waves and changed its aspect, the flat-topped purple wall being transmuted into brown, rugged, perpendicular cliffs, crowned with dark green foliage. Passing as we did close in by the extreme northern point, we were impressed by its beauty and grandeur, which far exceeds even that of the cliffs at Mount Desert. Then came the Bishop's Head, presenting the rude outline of what appears like a tonsured monk sitting in a chair. It is not so definite in its outline as the Friar's Head at Campo Bello, yet, taken altogether, it surpasses it by far. A little further on is Eel Brook Cove, with its fine rocky cliffs. At this place the ship Lord Ashburton was wrecked. Several of the crew were saved, yet the marvel is how they got up the steep rocks. In the graveyard near Flagg's Cove, the bodies of twenty-one of the unfortunates lie side by side.

In a few minutes we dashed gaily into Whale Cove, a broad bay in the form of a horse-shoe, indenting the northern end of the island. Here the view is surprisingly fine, the entire shore being circled by immense cliffs that rise up around the border of the blue waves, with a richness of color and stateliness of aspect that cannot fail to impress the beholder.

But we had no time now to stay and study the cliffs in detail, as our destination was Flagg's Cove, and we were in doubt about its precise locality. We accordingly ran down to a fishing boat, and, on inquiry, learned that the cove in question made in on the eastern side of the island, extending to within a quarter of a mile of Whale Cove. Our skipper had contracted to carry us to the former place, but as the night was coming on, and he was anxious to get the breeze home again, we released him from the bargain and were put ashore. On the whole it was best, and persons coming as we did, will generally do well to land here; that is, of course, if the surf should not prove high. The northerly gales, it will be remembered, drive directly upon the land.

Our craft was brought to close by the shore, and we reached the beach in a dory. Some fishermen were dressing hake near their boat-houses, and two or three small boys were at play. Our arrival attracted the latter, who at once came down to us. As I jumped upon the soil of the Dominion, I addressed one of the brightest of them, saying that I supposed he was one of Victoria's boys. To this he snarled a most emphatic "No." I told him that he need not feel ashamed of so sweet a lady and so good a Queen; yet for all that he said nay. It was the blood of Cape Cod and Cape Ann that colored his freckled face; the same that coursed in the veins of the old privateersmen. What saith the poet? *Cœlum non animum mutant, qui trans mare currunt;* which means that the Marbleheader may change skies and fishing grounds, but not his inveterate Yankee notions. Still we are supposed here to be under the protection of Her Majesty's Flag, and so, God save the Queen. To which Amarinta, stepping ashore, says, Amen, preferring the reign of Victoria much before that of Neptune.

Next we arranged with the fishermen to carry our baggage across to Flagg's Cove, as soon as they had pickled their last hake, then bade our trusty skipper good-by, and started on ahead through a lane, passing a couple of fishermen's cottages, the graves of the Ashburton's crew, the school-house with a belfry and rat-tail spire, and the bulging sides of the new town hall, to which the scarcity of the public funds cruelly denies a roof. In due time I found the house to which I had been recommended by an artist of New York, who had spent three summers here, and which others may also readily find without any public mention of names. Leaving wave-tossed Amarinta to recover from the lunging of the great herring-boat, let us take a glance at the earlier days of Grand Menan.

Menan is an Indian word signifying an island. The Passamaquoddy Indians, in response to my inquiries when at their village, gave me several words of a similar sound, which all have the same signification. The island first appears in the voyage of Champlain in 1605. He speaks of it as the island called by the savages *Manthane*. He is careless in the spelling of this and many other proper names. In another instance he calls it *Manasne*. He anchored once near its southern head. Down to the period of the Revolution, it appears to have been inhabited only by the Indians. A farmer near Eel Brook gave me a stone chisel that belonged to the aborigines. It was ploughed up in a field. During the Revolution the Indians who resorted hither were allied to the American cause. Colonel John Allan, who in 1777 conducted operations in Eastern Maine, appears to have had more or less connection with them. He speaks in his journal of sending off Indians to this place, and also of issuing orders for their return. In December, he sent Ensign Smith to Grand Menan, but it was the old story, "not being able from bad weather to proceed." If any white men settled here prior to the declaration of peace, there is no record of the fact accessible.

According to the best authority to be had just now, one of the earliest settlers on the island was Moses Gerrish, of Massachusetts, who adhered to the King when the Revolution broke out, and was attached to the commissary department of the royal army. After the peace, in connection with Thomas Ross and John Jones, he obtained license of occupation of this island, together with New Brunswick and its dependencies; and, on condition of obtaining forty settlers, a schoolmaster and clergyman, within seven years of the date of the license, they were to have a grant of the whole from the Crown. They sold lots in anticipation of the title, but in the end failed to get the grant. Jones returned to the United States, and Gerrish and Ross remained. Gerrish, according to Sabine, who gives these facts, possessed some ability. He was described by one individual as a man who " would spread more good sense on a sheet of paper" than any person of his acquaintance. Still he was not very persistent, and never amassed any property. He was always *going* to do something. He was a magistrate at Menan at the time of his death, which took place in 1830, in the eightieth year of his age.

The first habitations were very rude, but the people have continued to improve the character of their dwellings, until they compare very favorably with structures of a corresponding character on the coast of Maine.

The island itself is about twenty-two miles long and from three to six miles wide. It lies in the mouth of the Bay of Fundy, anciently called Frenchman's Bay. The furious tide for which this bay is distinguished, sweeps by the shores with great force, rising eighteen feet on the west side and seventeen on the east.

The highest part of the island is at its northern end, where the cliffs rise four hundred feet, gradually sloping as they extend southward, where, at the terminus, they are three hundred feet high. The land also descends eastward until in the middle portions it sinks under the sea. If the water among the islands on the south side were filled up, Grand Menan would form a triangular-shaped body of land; but then the east coast would be as destitute of harbors as the west. As it remains, the eastern shore affords many

Grand Menan. 247

facilities to the shipping. There are no cliffs on this side, except at the northern end, and in one or two places towards the south. The villages and roads are, of course, confined to the east side. Only a few narrow cart-tracks extend to the west side, which is generally reached by going through the woods on foot.

At the present time the inhabitants number about eighteen hundred. There are not less than four hundred dwelling-houses and five hundred buildings of all other kinds. There are five societies of Baptists, and a Church of England Parish. This is at Grand Harbor. The schools at present number only three, though, according to a legal provision, they may have seven. The inhabitants maintain a military organization. The only taxes paid are for the county and the poor. These are moderate. They hold public meetings, and make their own local laws without let or hindrance, and vote for whomsoever they please to represent them in Parliament. The government is liberal everyway, appropriating a certain sum annually for the repair of roads, and selling the public lands to any one who will buy them at a low figure and pay the price by building a road to his own door. It would do some of our blatant Republican friends who indulge in so much spread-eagleism on the Fourth of July, to come down to Grand Menan and view these institutions for themselves. On the other hand, certain of the grumbling Menanites would do well to throw their nets for a season in the waters of Massachusetts Bay, where the Cape Codder is taxed thirty dollars in the thousand to keep his sandy roads from being devoured by the wind, and where the State and National dues make men sick even to think of them. Happy Menanites, who, free from grinding taxation, now rove out from rock-bound coves, and quarry at will in the silvery mines of the sea!

But this is not all. Trade is absolutely *free*. Here no smuggler waits the favorable tide, or the oblivious fog, to run his contraband canoe into solitary nooks and creeks, as at Campo Bello and Lubec. No descendant of Matthew the Publican sits at the receipt of Customs to ask the nature of his freight. This port is open to every market of the world. From silk to nutmeg all is free. Dainty damsels can buy their kids at prices fabulously low, while some besides Dives know that purple and fine linen may be economically worn. But, speaking of kids, they are not much needed here. Buckskin, for the hands, is better, while among the cliffs the feet should be iron-shod.

The great attraction of Grand Menan, is the cliffs. Of mountains there are none. The place is altogether unlike Mount Desert. As has already been said, when seen from the main, it appears perfectly flat. Not a hummock breaks the entire line of wall. Among these cliffs we daily went a "cruising," as our landlady termed it, in the vernacular of the place.

An ordinary cliff is a fine thing. To see the living rock that has been rent in twain by convulsions, lifting high up its scarred front, maintaining an immovable calm both in sunshine and storm, is always impressive; but when the cliff is brought out on such a stupendous scale as at Grand Menan, with all the accessories of a wild ocean shore, the interest becomes absorbing. The other parts of the island are of course invested with much interest. The low eastern shore, fringed with small islands and rocks, affords many beautiful sights. In a pleasant day, a walk southward has many charms. The bright sky, the shingle beach, the picturesque boats, and blue landlocked bays continually enforce the admiration of an artistic eye, and allure the pedestrian on past cape, cove and reach, until he suddenly finds that miles of ground intervene between him and his dinner.

But whoever comes here will desire to traverse the entire island and visit the regions around the southern head. Starting from Flagg's Cove, the first four miles carry us over a hard road, as good as the drives in an ordinary park, which skirts the shores of Long Island Bay, and leaving us at Woodward's Cove. Besides the village meeting house, a second is passed during this stage of the journey, in addition to a small chapel; for whatever else there may be wanting here, there is no lack of ecclesiastical establishments. At the cove there is a post office and various herring establishments, as well as a collection of dwellings. Three miles farther on is Grand Cove, a spacious but shallow harbor. Here is the English Church, a plain structure of stone, with no special attractions of any sort to render it interesting. Ritualism has never invaded its walls, and a good portion of one end is filled up by an enormous pulpit and reading desk of a pattern suggestive of Noah's Ark. Opposite the church is the school-house. I stopped here when riding down the island and picked up a supply of ammunition to salute the village curs that snapped at our nag's heels; and at the same time stopped at the school-room to make some inquiries about the route. The pedagogue was within, seated upon his throne, instructing the young idea how to shoot, surrounded by about twenty unkempt boys. We were invited to walk in and view the school; but as we had a long ride before us we thanked the master and declined the invitation for the time. We then left the line of the shore altogether, and struck through a new road, running over a piece of marshy land covered with young trees, and continued until we reached Seal Cove, which is five miles farther on the way. Here a brook empties into a wee harbor, the mouth of which is nearly closed up by a wharf. Small vessels, however, manage to squeeze in, and lie in safety. From thence for some distance the road is quite hilly. On its most elevated part was another Baptist meeting house. It being an unusually warm day for Grand Menan, a flock of sheep had assembled in its shade. They found it grateful. Farther on we had a view of the ocean and the neighboring isles, while at the same time the woods retreated and left an open down sprinkled with sheep. The prospect here reminded me of some lines from Dyer:

> " Such are the downs of Banstead, edg'd with woods,
> And tow'ry villas; such Dorcestrian fields,
> Whose flocks innum'rous whiten all the land;
> Such those slow climbing wilds, that lead the step
> Insensibly to Dover's windy cliff.
> Tremendous height! and such the clovered lawns
> And sunny mounts of beauteous Normanton."

Crossing this place we descended when the road again returned to the line of the shore, which here holds up to the sea a high perpendicular wall. At the end of fourteen miles from Flagg's Cove, we reached the house of Mr. Walter B. McLaughlin, a son of an old Waterloo veteran, and one of the live men of Menan. Here, like Goldsmith's broken soldier, we were "kindly bade to stay," and accepted an invitation to pass the night.

Mr. McLaughlin is the keeper of the famous Gannet Rock Lighthouse, and holds other appointments under the Dominion. Thoroughly true to Her Majesty, the Queen, he is at the same time heartily in sympathy with the loyal people of the United States, and intelligently follows them in all their conflicts. The lighthouse of which he has the charge may be seen in clear weather, a mere speck out at sea. It stands upon a small rock, just large enough to receive the establishment, which combines beacon and dwelling in one. Access to the rock can be had only in calm weather, consequently in the winter season, in company with his family, he is a fast prisoner, not having so much as a foot of ground to walk on, and the waves ever thundering against the wall. It being fine weather, I chanced to find him ashore, directing his haying, and obtained some of the local statistics. The situation of his *land* home is extremely fine, as the breakers dash continually against the rocks only a few yards from the door.

Two miles further south is Deep Cove, where a brawling, dark-brown brook comes out through an opening in a sea-wall thrown up by the waves across its mouth. From this point the road goes on but a short distance before it terminates. The pedestrian must then push on through paths for the rest of the distance to the Southern Head. Here he will come upon the cliffs, and find the rocks thrown up in the wildest confusion. Pintor and his friend found much sameness in them as rock studies. One of the most remarkable objects here is an isolated rock, or drong, resembling the figure of a colossal woman. It is known as the Old Maid, and is found on the west side of the head. It excites more admiration than the general class known by the name. It has no tongue. The other principal point of interest found in this vicinity is Bradford's Cove. It is reached by a path through the woods. In an easterly gale it is a place of safety, yet at the time of our visit the masts of a lost ship, the Mavoureen, were seen rising just above the top of the waves. Around the cliffs of the Southern Head is a favorite nesting place for the gulls, which lay their gray eggs, splashed with brown, in rude nests, contrived with little care among the grass. They are also found in one or two of the islands near by. The Indians take the young gulls and carry them away. I saw several of them at Pleasant Point that had been thus torn from the parental nest at Grand Menan. They were tamer than chickens, and were being fattened on porpoise for some future feast.

Audubon visited Grand Menan in May, 1833, and landed at White Head Island, the property of Mr. Frankland, where he inspected the herring gulls, then breeding in great numbers. His account of these birds is of much interest. He says: " We immediately set out in search of them, directing our course toward the pine wood, in which we were informed we should find them. As we came up to the place I observed that many of the gulls had alighted on the fir trees, while a vast number were sailing around, and when we advanced, the former took to wing, abandoning their nests and all flew about uttering incessant cries. I was greatly surprised to see the nests placed on branches, some near the top, others about the middle or on the lower parts of the trees, while at the same time there were many on the ground. It is true I had been informed of this by our captain, but

I had almost believed that on arriving at the spot I should find the birds not to be gulls. My doubts, however, were now dispelled, and I was delighted to see how nature had provided them with the means of securing their eggs from their arch-enemy, man. My delight was greatly increased on being afterwards informed by Mr. Frankland that the strange habit in question had been acquired by the gulls within his recollection; for, said he, 'when I first came here, many years ago, they all built their nests on the moss and in open ground; but as my sons and the fishermen collected most of their eggs for winter use, and sadly annoyed the poor things, the old ones gradually began to put up their nests on the trees in the thickest part of the woods. The youngest birds, however, still have some on the ground, and on the whole are becoming less wild since I have forbidden strangers to rob their nests; for, gentlemen, you are the only persons out of my family that have fired a gun on White Head Island for several years past.' I was much pleased with the humanity of our host, and requested him to let me know when all the gulls, or the greater part of them would abandon the trees and resume their former mode of breeding on the ground, which he promised to do. But I afterwards found that this was not likely to happen, because on some other islands not far distant, to which the fishermen and eggers have free access, these gulls breed altogether on the trees, even when their eggs and young are regularly renewed every year, so that their original habits have been entirely given up. Some of the nests which I saw were placed at the height of more than forty feet on the trees; others, seen in the thickest part of the woods, were eight or ten feet from the ground, and were placed close to the main stem, so as to be with difficulty observed. It was truly curious to see the broad-winged birds make their way to and from them in these secluded retreats. The nests placed on the ground were several yards apart, and measured from fifteen to eighteen inches in diameter, their cavity being from four to six. The lower stratum consisted of grass, plants of various kinds, moss and grey lichens, and the whole was lined with fine bent, but without any feathers. Those on the trees measured from twenty-four to twenty-six inches in diameter externally, and were composed of the same material, but in greater quantity, the object of which I thought might be to allow more space to the young while growing, as they could enjoy the pleasure of running about like those hatched on the ground. Perhaps, however, the smaller size of the nests placed there may be owing to their belonging to the younger gulls, as I have often observed that the older the individual the larger is the nest. About the beginning of May the Herring gulls collect into great flocks for the purpose of reproducing, and betake themselves to the large sand-bars or mud-flats at low water. With the aid of a glass you may see them going through their courtships; the males swell their throats, walk proudly about, throw their heads upwards, and emit their love notes. These general meetings take place at all hours of the day according to the state of the tide, and continue for about a fortnight, when they all depart and betake themselves to the island where they breed."

Leaving this part of Grand Menan with many regrets, we returned to Flagg's Cove to examine that region with more care.

One day, when an easterly gale was blowing, Pintor and I improved the occasion to walk around Sprague's Cove and Swallow Tail Light. Three fourths of a mile northward brought us to the cliffs south of the cove, and following these we reached the shore of the place in question. All the way along they are grandly shattered and wave-worn, presenting perfect pictures at every step. The sight of harebells and wild roses drenched by the salt spray, and still holding on against the gale in some crevice half way down the cliff, taught a lesson of confidence.

Sprague's Cove itself presents the most complete view of a fishing hamlet that I have anywhere found. Everything likewise appears to have been arranged for artistic effect. The old boats, the tumble-down store-houses, the picturesque costumes, the breaking surf, and all the miscellaneous paraphernalia of such a place, set off as they are by the noble back-ground of richly-colored cliffs, produce an effect that is as rare as beautiful. Certainly no artist should undertake to depict scenes of this character before he has studied Sprague's Cove. We viewed it in all its aspects on this stormy day, noted the best points to sketch from the coming summer; and then began to climb the south side of Swallow Tail Head, which here spreads out eastward into the sea, taking the form of the caudal appendage belonging to the said bird. The tide being down, we first passed through a huge passage eaten out of a projecting bastion of the cliff. Afterwards we climbed straight up over the fallen rocks. When half way up we looked back and saw in the face of the cliff through which we had passed, a striking profile that bore so strong a resemblance to the face of Washington that we knew Victoria would not object for a moment to our naming it "Washington's Cliff." This we did, and so, gentle reader, when you go to Sprague's Cove next summer, please use your (potent) influence to help make the name stick.

Nearing the top of the cliff, we began to understand how one or two men of the Ashburton's crew got up Eel Brook rocks; for, when within a few feet of the top, the force of the gale well nigh lifted us up, without any effort on our part. Once on the top, we walked along on the greensward out towards the light-house, breasting the heavy gale. The point upon which it stands is separated from the rest of the head by a horrid chasm, crossed by a narrow bridge. There is first a steep descent, before the bridge can be reached. To make this safe, an anchor with a rope attached is planted in the ground at the top. Holding firmly to this, we cautiously went down and crossed the bridge, all the while with the gale tugging at our legs and trying to carry them off. Passing the lighthouse and climbing out to the extremity of the rocks, Pintor inserted himself in a crevice, like a hermit-crab in his shell, and made several pencil sketches, one of which was a fishing schooner under double reefs, beating around into the cove. The skipper's quick eye detected us in our hiding-places, as his vessel passed under the cliffs, pitching like a porpoise, and held on to the main shrouds while he swung his "sou'wester" for a salute. In the evening he came ashore to our cottage, and regaled us with the account of the wonderful "sea-serpent," which had just been captured (by the newspapers) at Lake Utopia, together with the account of the serpent at Eagle Lake in Mount Desert, which has already been referred to. In the midst of this gale a fishing vessel was out all day on the "Ripplings," a dangerous place several miles at sea, where they seined forty barrels of herring. Such facts tell us something of the great courage and uncompromising perseverance of these fishermen, who constantly brave danger in every form.

Leavitt, in one of his poems, gives us an admirable picture of the scene at Swallow-Tail Light in a stormy day:

> "The picture view! what wild sublimity!
> Omnipotence has waked and hurl'd the storm,
> Tossing the deep to tumult. Round that tower,
> Rising defiant on its ocean-rock,
> Dashes the maniac wave, whose flying spray
> Hung high in air, before the tempest streams,
> While seabirds circle on exultant wing,
> Silent and calm, above the roar and foam
> Of battling elements."

Another point at this end of the island that will bear repeated visits is Whale Cove, where we first landed. The shingle beach extends entirely across the bottom of the cove, and is very high and broad. Originally the water extended nearly, if not quite through, to Flagg's Cove, where the ground is now occupied by a meadow. But the waves, in their haste to swallow up the land, quite defeated themselves, and in their fury threw up a barrier which they could not overpass; thus illustrating the habits of those men who always stand in the way of their own advancement.

On this beach are found some extremely fine pebbles of porphyry, jasper, and agate, besides other minerals that the collectors will be glad to bring away. In clear calm weather this place has a wonderful attraction. On the east side is Fish Head, and on the west Eel Brook and Northern Head, the latter extending out beyond its neighbor, and between are the blue sky and water. At low tide, the uncovered beach allows the rambler to stray as far as Eel Cove, but it is idle to attempt to go farther, without ascending the cliffs and following along the escarpment. Starting from Whale Cove, we found the line of cliffs continually rising. Its geological character is also variable. A large portion of the rock shows signs of stratification, but there are also immense masses of trap-rock, a great deal of which takes the basaltic character of Giant's Causeway, the regularly-formed columns standing closely packed. Among the trap-rock we found small specimens of native copper. Masses of this material, of a dozen pounds weight, have been found in the fields above the shore. One of the natives, who saw us hammering among the rocks, seemed to think that we were speculators spying out the land. He accordingly took an ax, came after us, and rendered good service in splitting open the trap. If anything was going on, he evidently wanted to have a hand in it, and to share the prize. Eventually he concluded that we knew no more about what was to be found in the rocks than he did. Assured of this, he returned to swing a scythe in a neighboring field.

On one of those extremely foggy days, such as occur here too often, Pintor and I took a long ramble under the cliffs among the slippery rocks that lie at their base, and found it a fatiguing work, though we thought it *paid*. This time we had none of those

"Blue-hayred defs
That drearie hang o'er Dover's emblaunched clefs,"

Grand Menan. 261

but the genuine Menan fog, direct from the Grand Bank. It was so dense as to be perfectly oppressive, while the line of vision was bounded by the escarpment of the cliffs and the breaking surf close by on the shore. We could not see the ocean, yet from out an impenetrable vail it launched its booming thunder, rolling sullenly against these long adamantine walls, and filling us at times with a kind of indefinable dread and awe. Still, we knew the ways of the tide, and felt confident that there was no danger to be apprehended from the "bore," which, higher up the Bay of Fundy, puts men on the seashore in peril of their lives. Therefore, we scrambled on among the rocks and heaps of drift-wood, of which there is enough on every beach to gladden the hearts of all the poor widows in New York. As we passed along, we noted the place where two waterfalls ordinarily belong. Only *one* was now to be seen coming down the cliff, reduced almost to a thread, and spinning itself into a veil of airy lace before reaching the bot-bottom. I consoled myself for the failure of the water with a reflection of Dr. Johnson at the empty Fall of Tiers—Nature never gives everything at once. Here we turned and pursued the homeward way, leaving the cliffs behind us like grand melancholy ghosts, doomed to haunt the fog forever.

It was a far different day that we dedicated to Indian Beach, on the west side of the island, and the resort of the Passamaquoddy Indians. It is full four miles from Flagg's Cove, and in going thither it will not prove amiss to take a boat at Whale Cove and sail around, on account of the difficulty of the walk. Amarinta, Pintor and I took a wagon as far as the head of Eel Brook, where the road running across the island ends. The rest of the journey was done on foot. From the end of the road we moved westward and crossed Eel Brook, a stream that runs from its source in a little lake near by, to the cove, where it is lost in the sea. At the brook is a little mill, one of eleven that in the wet season do the sawing of Menan. The rest of the way to the shore lies through a woodpath, where we found several of the bark lodges that form the winter camps of the Indian hunter. There is still considerable game here, though for the past three years the hunting of deer has been strictly prohibited. But Indians, and certain of the inhabitants, have no regard for the law. There is quite a large number of deer on the island. Our landlady told us that the previous summer she suddenly came face to face with one of the e antlered beauties, who, after looking at her until he was throroughly satisfied, turned and capered away into the woods. Mr. Gerrish, the old settler already alluded to, brought a pair of moose to the island and dismissed them to the woods. In course of time they multiplied to such an extent that moose were quite plenty. In 1818 no less than a dozen were killed. They have now become extinct.

Notwithstanding the distance from the mainland, the deer occasionally swim across to find a refuge from the dogs, who are feared more than the surging sea. Of the fact itself there can be no doubt. If Leander swam the Hellespont for his love, what may not a powerful deer do for his life? Still, it is after all difficult to conceive of the exact mental state of an animal that plunges into the surf at West Quoddy, and breasts the furious tide to reach the low purple wall that he discovers nine miles over the waves. How does he know that there is land there? He may scent it, but do not conclude that he knows it, though his eye may be more telescopic than ours. This perhaps is the solution: as a drowning man catches at a straw, so a hotly-pressed buck, hearing the panting of the hound, accepts what resembles the Highlands of Neversink as a sanctuary. He is a quick-witted, sensible creature, and when he sees that he has but one chance, he takes that one chance, and makes the most of it. The crew of the Revenue Cutter lately caught a noble fellow in this identical mood, when he was about half-way over, and hauled him on board. I did not hear the sequel; but let us picture the jolly tars as endowed with their traditional generosity, which leads them to admire courage in misfortune, and not less kind than the sea. As for the Indians, they have as little regard for mercy as for law; and, statute or no statute, they will have the venison and pelt. In these little lodges that we were just speaking of, they crouch around the fire kindled in the middle on the ground, and doom the gentle fawns to death. We looked into several and found the forked sticks that serve as pot-hooks still suspended from above. The coming winter they will doubtless return, and then more than one desperate buck will take his death-leap down the cliffs of Grand Menan.

Passing these lodges, the path eventually ends in the open fields near the cliffs, and here is a most convenient break, where we descended to the beach. This place is known as Long's Eddy, as the tide sees fit, on reaching this part of the coast, to imitate the playfulness of a kitten chasing her tail. Here, too, the herring sports in search of smaller fry, which become his prey. But the herring, in turn, becomes the prey of the porpoise, and the porpoise the prey of the Indian, and the Indian the prey of the oil factor. Where the law of retribution ends I cannot say, but sometimes it certainly reaches the dupes in the grease department of Wall Street.

From this point the way was open northward along the beach to the fine crags of Bishop's Head. Close by, a shingle beach projects like a flattened V, leaving behind it, at the foot of the cliffs, a small lake, on the border of which, within the reach of the salt spray, were several flourishing firs. It was very trustful in the trees to grow here.

Opposite, towards the mainland, we saw where the

Fenians, during their invasion, sunk a vessel; and looking southward along the coast, a white beach glimmered in the afternoon sun. We judged it a mile and a half distant, and set out to walk there, as the tide was now far enough down. The first half of the distance was easily accomplished, as there is a broad strip of beach covered with small stones, but the rest of the distance is extremely hard. As we were plodding along, a whale—

> " Leviathan, which God of all His works
> Created hugest that swim the ocean stream,"

vouchsafed to pay his respects, rearing his dark sides above the waves with infinite ease and grace.

Nearing our destination, the difficulties of the route increased, as the shore was piled with boulders varying in size from a barrel to a small cottage, many of which were moist and slippery. It was a severe trial for Amarinta, and our slow progress enabled Pintor, who was more nimble of foot, to stop occasionally and sketch the forms of the rocks, which are magnificently colored, and great treasures for a sea-side painter.

Finally every difficulty was passed, and we stepped upon the smooth shore of Indian Beach. Here are the lodges of the Indians, built chiefly of bark, and kept in place by large stones laid on the roofs and against the sides. It was a windy afternoon and unfit for porpoise hunting.

It has been already stated that these Indians belong

to the Passamaquoddy tribe about whom some facts may not prove unacceptable. Father Vetromile says that the name is a corruption of Peskamaquontik, from the name Peskadaminkkanti, *it goes up into the open field*, and not from the word Quoddy, *haddock*, as commonly supposed. Their ancient village was on the British territory now occupied by St. Andrews. They lost their lands, and for some time led a roving life, but finally land was granted them at *Sybaik*, Pleasant Point, Maine. This is about five miles above Eastport, though a small company afterward fixed their abode at Lewis' Island. The latter belong to the so-called "New Party," which sprang into existence during a controversy about their governor or chief. They number about four hundred and forty, and draw an annuity from the government. Their houses are comfortably built, though not in all cases neatly kept. At the time I visited their village the house of the governor was undergoing repairs, and the Indians had also completed a "hall," which they use for dancing, an amusement of which they are immoderately fond, and in which both grown persons and children indulge until the small hours come, animated by a fiddle or fife.

The school, supported by the Board of Education, numbers about thirty-five scholars, but when I looked into the school-house there were only five or six present. The master apologized for the thin attendance, saying that they all went to the dance the previous night. It is impossible to put them under any set discipline. About eleven o'clock, the scholars, many of whom are twenty years old, began to come in one by one, looking tired and sleepy. They study little, but make up for their lack of industry by giggling. It is impossible to force them. Yet some are quite proficient, and the master called upon one bright looking little girl, whose English name was Mary, to spell some words in her Primer for the edification of Amarinta and myself. But Mary was unused to strangers, and on being urged gently she hid her face in her hands and burst into tears. We were quite sorry for being the cause of grief, and tried all manner of blandishments to win her confidence, including a lavish outlay of small coin; yet while prudently holding on to the cash with one hand she covered her face with the other, and was inconsolable. We gave it up at last and went to look into the church, dedicated to St. Anne. It is neat in its appearance, though profusely adorned with meretricious prints, such as find their way into the poorer class of Roman churches. Attached is a house for the priest. The Indians are, of course, devout Romanists, and several of their number have been made deacons; an office which they support in accordance with the Indian ideas of dignity and decorum. Their burying ground on the hill-side at Pleasant Point, presents those picturesque features which ordinarily belong to the aborigines who hold the Roman faith. Each grave is housed with wood, and huge crosses lift themselves up from afar. The branch which settled at Lewis' Island also have a church dedicated to St. Anne.

At all seasons of the year the people are more or less scattered, being engaged in hunting, fishing and basket-making. In the latter employment they do not excel. The Indian blood is by no means pure, being much corrupted by an infusion of French. But their faces are well bronzed, and the most of them are sufficiently savage in their aspect. But let us return to Menan.

Here on the beach we found quite a colony. A part of them spoke English. Their canoes, finely built, and worth from twenty-five to fifty dollars apiece, were drawn up in a row on the sand. Some of the men were trying out porpoise oil, and others were making or repairing the various implements of their craft; while several children were playing with dogs. It was a novel scene, indeed, with the noble back-ground of cliffs crowned with dark green foliage. Pintor accordingly pulled out his sketch book, and rapidly transferred the picture to its pages, a knot of these savages all the while looking over his shoulder, and expressing their admiration or surprise with a grunt. For myself I made inquiries about the porpoises and the mode of catching them, while Amarinta spake with the women concerning baskets.

Their custom is to shoot them with a rifle, and,

before they have time to sink, paddle up and make fast with a lance, when the creature is dead taking him into the canoe. I afterwards saw them at their work. One Indian sat at the stern of the canoe, using his paddle as easily as a fish does his fins, and another, rifle in hand, stood at the bow. And who is this dark complexioned, small bodied, but firmly knit Indian, with an eye like a snake, stealthily searching the waves for his prey and clutching his rifle with such a significant grasp? I *thought* I had seen him before. This is the Reverend Tomma Denni, Deacon of the Holy Roman Catholic Church. If he could scent a heresy as he tracks a porpoise, he would answer as an examiner of the Inquisition. Pity the porpoise upon whom he "draws a bead," for he is as good as in the try-pot. The Reverend Tomma fishes for both porpoises and men.

Some distance south is Dark Cove, a place marked by many romantic features. The harbor, formed by the sea wall, is about a mile long, and half a mile wide. In 1846 a channel was cut, when the sea rushed in with a loud roar and raised the level of the water eight feet, giving, ordinarily, a depth of from five to nine fathoms. On the landward side of the harbor is a clearing of fifty acres. In 1852 one John Sinclair had been living in this lonely spot for quarter of a century. Vessels can enter the harbor at about two hours from high water. Here they lie in perfect safety. This is a lumbering station, and has few residents, except at the busy season of the year. The path thither lies through the woods, and, nearer at hand, is Money Cove, where search has been made for the treasures of the inevitable Kidd, who was sacrificed by the politicians to save the reputation of Lord Somers and the Earl of Bellomont, and whom popular tradition wrongly represents as a common, blood-thirsty pirate. The old song does not even give Kidd's *name* correctly, (much less any true idea of his character), making him say—

"My name was *Robert* Kidd, as I sailed,"

instead of William.

At this place a brook flows down between two cliffs, and a couple of old wells are thought to belong to some ancient French settlers.

It was impossible to visit these places now, and therefore we cast about us to devise our return. At this juncture a lucky thought occurred to Amarinta. The Indians should carry us back to Long's Eddy in a canoe. It would save that climb among the rocks, and be *so* romantic. A bargain was therefore struck on the spot, two Indians then carried down a canoe, Pintor put his sketch-book in his pocket, and we all carefully got aboard, stowing ourselves away at the bottom. One of our copper-colored brethren sat in the bows and braced up the mast which had a large spritsail attached, while the other steered and held the sheet in his hand. A fresh breeze was now blowing along the shore, and no sooner was the canoe free from the beach than it flew away before the wind like an arrow. This was really more like sailing than anything I had ever experienced before in my life, and we glided almost noiselessly for a mile and a half, with nothing but a thin piece of birch-bark between us and the deep Bay of Fundy. The cliffs went past as the railway stations flit by an express train, and before we were aware of the fact the canoe safely touched the shore at Long's Eddy.

As a place of summer resort, Grand Menan is in some respects unequalled. At certain seasons the fog is abundant, yet that can be endured. Here the opportunities for recreation are unlimited, and all persons fond of grand seashore views may indulge their taste without limit.

The people are invariably kind and trustworthy, and American manners and habits prevail to such an extent that travellers at once feel at home. They generally take a lively interest in American affairs, and are well informed on the principal political questions. During the late Rebellion many "skedadlers," as the Menanites call them, took refuge here, generally coming over in stolen boats. They were not highly respected, and the general opinion is that they stole about as many boats when they left as when they came.

This will never become a fashionable resort. The magnificent Mrs. All-pork, of All-pork Place, would take little comfort here. Her trains would not draggle well among the rocks, and she would ask to go home by the first boat. Yet persons of refined taste, who desire to escape from the stereotyped insipidity of the fashionable watering place, and are willing to take such fare as the island affords, may spend a pleasant month here in the summer. For a number of years it has been a favorite haunt of artists, as the walls of the Academy bear witness. The albums of the young ladies hereabouts are full of their photographs, all the prominent artists of the country being represented. As some may feel curious on the subject of expense, I may mention that six or seven dollars is the ordinary fare from Boston, and that half-a-dollar a day in gold will cover the cost of diet, such as it is.

But our sojourn in this paradise of cliffs came to an end, and we were obliged to leave. So, the reader may perhaps desire to know how we got back to the mainland. We had expected to take the Wednesday packet, but fearing that the wind might not serve, we left on the Monday previous. About nine o'clock we went down to the beach and saw a vessel sailing out of the cove, and learned that she was bound to Eastport. The wind was light, and therefore could we overtake her in a row-boat?

Then spake Goodman Stanton, a fisherman of curious genealogy, in whom Cape Cod, Cape Ann and Mount Desert were wondrously mixed up, and who often unconsciously posed for the artists visiting the shore. We could hardly catch the vessel now from this place, but if we started off to Whale Cove, we might get aboard when she came around from Swallow Tail Head; very likely we could. And he guessed that they would stop and take us aboard.

It was a beautiful day for the voyage, and so I soon packed up, put Amarinta and the luggage into the wagon, started off old Roan limping towards the cove; and, bidding our kind landlady adieu, followed after on foot, leaving our artist-friends to bring up the rear.

Before all the party reached the shore of the cove, the breeze sprang up, and the expected vessel came in sight, passing on her way. I accordingly started a couple of fishermen in a light boat to head her off, and persuade the skipper to wait. The schooner was now a full mile from shore, but they sprang to their work and were soon half-way out, when they stopped, put their jackets on their oars, and waved them as a signal, hallooing at the same time with all their might. Of this the skipper took no notice and sailed merrily on his way. Again, therefore, they plied the oars, and at the end of another quarter of a mile stopped and went through a still more lunatic performance. This was too much for the skipper, and he accordingly hove to and waited for them to come alongside. Then we saw the boat leave them, and the schooner headed off once more on the course to Eastport. We now thought that our embassy had failed; but it turned out that Goodman Stanton knew best; for as soon as the schooner got steerage way again, the skipper put the helm down, brought his craft to, hauled the jib-sheet to the windward, and so wore round and stood for the shore. In ten minutes more we were all on the deck of the *Flash*, an English fishing smack of thirty tons, bound for a cargo of salt. At the helm stood a middle-aged man with a curious droop about one eye, whom I took for a well-to-do factor of fish; but I (mentally) cried his mercy when I happened to discover that, instead, he was a fisher of men. Yesterday, with the form of sound words, and in some one of the ecclesiastical centres of the island, he had divided the attention of certain Menanites with a Mormon elder, who was abroad even here doing the bidding of his master at Salt Lake.

The deck was covered with barrels of herring, but we found room to bestow ourselves upon the trunks. Contrary to our expectations, the breeze held fresh, and the schooner sailed swiftly past the headlands for the east side of Campo Bello. On our way we had one of the finest exhibitions of *mirage* ever witnessed on this coast, which has already been referred to in the chapter on fog. In three hours we were at the mouth of Eastport harbor, when the favorable tide caught us and swept us swiftly up to the town.

Our trip from the Isles of Shoals to Grand Menan is now ended; but next to the satisfaction taken in writing these notes will be the pleasure of doing it over again; for scenes like those through which we have wandered can never cloy, but will retain a perrenial freshness after repeated visits and the lapse of years.

APPENDIX.

I.

THE FRENCH SETTLEMENT.

Since the body of this work was completed, the journals and miscellaneous collections of General De Peyster, relating to Mount Desert, have been placed by him at our disposal. A much better use could have been made of this material if received sooner. I will, nevertheless, extract a few things of antiquarian interest.

General De Peyster, who has already been mentioned in connection with "The Dutch in Maine," visited Mount Desert in the years 1856-7. On reaching South-west Harbor he experienced the disappointment often felt by those who begin their acquaintance with the island there. Certain things, he thought, reminded him of the Mediterranean, and he admitted even that Somes' Sound was magnificent. On the whole, he thought that he should not care to stay more than a few days. In course of time, however, he changed his opinion, and when visiting Flying Mountain applauded the opinion of his Italian *Valet*, who exclaimed, "Italy ! Italy !"

General De Peyster's chief object while on the island was to find some relic of the Jesuit Mission. One day when on his way to Beech Mountain, General De Peyster says :

" We stopped at the house of old Mr. Isaac Mayhew, to ask him about the site of the first French settlement. He told me that when he came into this neighborhood with his father seventy-nine years ago, there was no difference of opinion with regard to the site of that colony. As I supposed, Flynn's Point was designated ; and he heard his father say that that was the point occupied. It is only recently that another generation pointed out other localities. * * * To my inquiry, did he ever hear of a settlement at North-east Harbor, he replied *no*, decidedly."

The General was also told " that the first French settlers cleared the ridge extending to the sea-wall and Flynn's Point; also that they occupied dwellings over the cellars and hearths still existing." Mr. Nicholas Thomas, who, while confined by an accident, wrote a history of his life in rhyme, gave him a great many stories, and, among others, one about a fort that was said to have existed on Flynn's Point.

" The fort," he says, " was built of wood, piled endwise, as if the open space was enclosed by a pile of cord-wood, by which expression, I suppose, it was intended to convey the meaning that the rampart was reveted in the same way that I have seen a bank kept up by refuse wood. This fort had embrasures, and mounted at least two guns, but of what calibre tradition does not state, though one *burst*, for his Uncle Mayhew told his father that he saw a piece of iron cannon dug up, part of the breech he thought, which weighed forty-four pounds."

Much time was also spent in directing exhumations at the various points suggested as sites occupied by the French, yet nothing satisfactory was found ; and finally an old inhabitant discouraged him from further efforts by assuring him that he knew the history of all the supposed relics which spade and pick brought up. The General therefore very wisely abandoned the work. He has, nevertheless, accumulated a large number of interesting traditions, and noted with much industry a great variety of valuable facts connected with the climate, topography, and the fisheries. His observations extend over the whole coast of Maine, and were originally collected with reference to publication.

Still every one must now concede, that the old men of Mount Desert have few qualifications as historians. They entertain the notion that the French made permanent settlements in 1613, and hence everywhere show relics of their occupation. But we have already demonstrated that the French did not remain over three months, and that their settlement at Fernald's Point was completely destroyed. Yet the inhabitants might well use their imaginations at a time when Bancroft's account, based on the prince of blunderers, Charlevoix, still disfigured his pages, and taught that the colony was located up the Penobscot. For a defence of Argall, see Massachusetts Historical Society's Collection, 1871.

II.
A FIGHT AT NORWOOD'S COVE.

To General De Peyster's journal I am indebted for the tradition in regard to a struggle at the above place in Somes' Sound, between the islanders and the British, during the Revolutionary war.

It appears, from the account, that the Captain of the British Frigate Tenedos undertook to cut out a couple of schooners at Norwood's Cove. At the time two companies of militia were stationed there, and when the British rowed in with their boats they opened fire, causing them to return to the Tenedos with considerable loss. It is said that the British buried their dead on Bear Island.

III.
TALLEYRAND AT MOUNT DESERT.

Griswold says in his *Republican Court:*

"It has been suggested that this extraordinary character was a native of Mount Desert, in Maine, and some curious facts have been adduced in support of this opinion. He had not long been in the country, before Mr. Edward H. Robbins, afterward Lieutenant Governor of Massachusetts, discovered him incog., at Mount Desert, wandering about without any apparent motive. The older inhabitants of that secluded place thought they recognized in him an illegitimate son of the pretty daughter of a fisherman and the captain of a French national ship which had been there in 1753. The boy, they said, when twelve or thirteen years of age, his mother being dead, had been taken away by a French gentleman, who declared that he was descended from a noble family in France. We may know about this in 1868, when the autobiography of the prince, acccecording to his last injunctions, will be published."—(p. 325.)

But we have heard of "old inhabitants" at this place before now, and their memories are certainly very faulty. Still it is an interesting question. McHarg's biography states that he was born in Paris, but cannot tell where, and says that it was reported that he never slept under his father's roof until he was twelve years old, and was totally neglected by his *reputed* mother. The publication of Talleyrand's Memoires have again been delayed, so that we shall get no light at present. Talleyrand, in his Essay on the Fisherman, *clearly* had the Mount Desert variety in mind.

IV.

ESTEVAN GOMEZ.

The earliest map showing any portion of the American coast was by Juan De La Cosa, of the date of A. D. 1500. The first printed map, that of John Ruysch, bears date of 1508, and is very rude. The most valuable is that of Ribero, of 1529, materials for which were furnished by Estevan Gomez, a Portuguese in the service of Spain, who discovered the Hudson River in 1525. This old map shows that Gomez was perfectly familiar with the Maine Coast, a fact that our historians appear not to have appreciated. On this ancient and invaluable map, which may be found in the collection of the unfortunate Lelewel, the coast from New York to Nova Scotia is called the *Land of Estevan Gomez.* The Penobscot is designated as "the River of Gomez," while other localities are easily recognized. This map, however, is not equal to Champlain's. The author does not remember a single writer who mentions Gomez in connection with Maine.

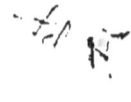

www.ingramcontent.com/pod-product-compliance
Lightning Source LLC
Chambersburg PA
CBHW032123230426
43672CB00009B/1841